'Scope Out Your Life

What your sign says about you

By Julia Marsden

This belongs
To megan

SCHOLASTIC INC.

New York Toronto London Auckland Sydney
Mexico City New Delhi Hong Kong

This book is dedicated to my Taurean monkey
and to all those who are inspired by the stars.

No part of this publication may be reproduced in whole or in part,
or stored in a retrieval system, or transmitted in any form or by any means,
electronic, mechanical, photocopying, recording, or otherwise, without
written permission of the publisher. For information regarding permission,
write to Petersen Publishing Company, L.L.C., 6420 Wilshire Boulevard,
Los Angeles, CA 90048-5515.

ISBN 0-439-15555-X

Copyright © 1999 by Petersen Publishing Co. All About You! is a trademark
of Petersen Publishing Company, L.L.C., and is used with permission.
All rights reserved. Published by Scholastic Inc., 555 Broadway, New York,
NY 10012, under license from Petersen Publishing Company. SCHOLASTIC
and associated logos are trademarks and/or registered trademarks of
Scholastic Inc.

12 11 10 9 8 7 6 5 4 3 2   0 1 2 3 4 5/0

Printed in the U.S.A.   01

First Scholastic Trade paperback printing, June 2000

Contents

Introduction

*H*ave you always been interested in astrology and want to learn more? Or have you always thought astrology seemed pretty cool but you don't have a clue? Well, either way, this book's for you. Reading your astro profile will give you insight into your sign's typical traits, strengths, and struggles. Plus, you'll learn more about your many moods and get clued in to why you react the way you do.

You'll also get the full scoop on the signs of your friends and family members. We don't advise bailing on any of your old buds, but check out The Friendship Factor chart and clue in to which zodiac signs you are most likely to click with.

This book's also packed with info about Chinese zodiac signs, moon signs, and numerology. So if you're all for learning about astrology, you're off to a great start!

Aries

The Ram
March 21–April 20

FAST FACTS ABOUT ARIES

You love: challenges, being seen as a leader, and taking initiative

Your key colors: red, black, and white

Your power flowers: red roses

Your star stones: diamonds and red jasper

Your metal: iron

Your astro animals: rams and sheep

Your day of the week: Tuesday

Your ruling planet: Mars, which symbolizes vitality, action, and a pioneering spirit

Your motto: I am.

AT YOUR BEST, you're seen as someone who is:

A leader
Energetic
Open to challenges
A risk taker
Persistent

AT YOUR WORST, you come across as someone who is:

Bossy
Brash
Selfish
Unwilling to listen to what others have to say
Opposed to being told what to do

YOUR SIGN IS ASSOCIATED WITH:

New beginnings
Exploration
Discovery
Competition
Courage

YOUR STELLAR STYLE

Ever been told you have a Type-A personality? It's a label that's given to people who are way beyond busy and always seem to be where the action is. Well, that *A* could definitely stand for Aries! Since your ruling planet is action-packed Mars, it's no wonder you're the girl who loves to take the lead! You really respond to opportunities to take charge, solve problems, and try new things. Not one to follow the crowd, you blaze your own trails and thrive on energy and independence. You've been known to avoid sticky or stressful situations by running away from them. But when you stick to your guns, you usually end up being the girl everyone turns to for answers.

WHAT YOU NEED TO SUCCEED

Here's a little something you might be too headstrong to admit: You need to know you're loved. While you may put up that "I'm too cool to be cuddled" front to your folks, if they offer you a hug, take it!

By cutting back on stuff that doesn't hold your interest and focusing on what matters to you most, you'll find a new sense of freedom. And by figuring out when it's best to act and when it's best to stay right where you are, you'll up the odds for being seen as the fearless leader you truly are. Also be prepared for one of your teachers to play an important role in your life.

FAMILY MATTERS

Beware of coming across as Miss Bossy! You pride yourself on knowing all the answers, but that doesn't mean others don't deserve a chance to be heard. Slow down long enough to listen. Practicing a little more patience with your parents will seriously help the situation on the home front. Like the other fire signs, Leo and Sagittarius, you're not exactly the Queen of Subtlety. You've been known to be a bit too blunt, but it's only because you like to let people know exactly how you feel. The cool thing about bluntness is that it often goes along with being very honest and straightforward.

STUDY STYLES THAT SUIT YOUR SIGN

If a subject is of interest to you, you're likely to ace it. Beware of being too rebellious around teachers who try your patience. Your headstrong habits can cause you to act out against authority figures (as in your beyond-boring music teacher). Just keep cool and concentrate on your schoolwork. Stick with subjects that give you a chance to express yourself. You're not exactly thrilled by tons of repetitious, detailed work. If an alternate assignment is an option, come up with something that'll let you showcase your awesome Aries creativity.

WHAT MAKES YOU A SOCIAL STAR

When it comes to hang time, you stick with a crowd that's all about being active and decisive. You value honesty in others and have been known to blow off anyone who tries to mislead you or hold you back from being your personal best. You have a true talent for making others feel at ease and have no problem being pals with people from every crowd. You're fiercely loyal to the friends who matter most to you and are the first to show up on the scene when a bud is feeling bad. Don't freak if your friends have a tendency to see you as the "leader of the pack" — that just means you're supertrue to your sign.

YOUR HEALTHY ASTRO ATTITUDE

Never ones to sit on the sidelines, those born under Aries are believed to be the natural athletes of the zodiac. When you zero in on your sport of choice, you're almost guaranteed to shine. Since you're big on doing your best, you may want to stick with a sport where you're a solo star, such as track-and-field events, gymnastics, ice-skating, swimming, diving, or singles tennis. However, your impulsive style can sometimes translate into sudden spurts of energy that can cause you to go so wacko with your workouts that you end up needing some serious couch-potato time! Strive to work out on a regular basis and steer clear of that all-or-nothing style. When stress strikes, do some stretches or pop in a yoga video to take the edge off.

FUTURE THINK

Since you're way into activity, being on the move, and taking initiative, a job that's pretty much the same old routine, day in and day out, is gonna drive you nuts. Look to head down a career track that'll keep you on the move. You may want to be your own boss so that what may seem like the slowpoke pace of others doesn't get you down. On the other hand, you'd be a great leader, director, or supervisor. Consider a career in the business world, politics, sports, or the military — anything that'll put you in charge!

ASTRO ADVICE ALWAYS

Spend the effort to make new friends.
Take advantage of the opportunity to travel and you'll discover a slew of new things.
Give a lot of thought to your future.

WINNING MOVES
FOR THE MONTHS AHEAD

You may have suffered some setbacks recently — doing a little advance planning could prevent the same snags from getting in your way again. Think before you act. Take a minute to picture how you want a particular situation to work out. Make a pact with yourself to learn from the lessons of the last few months. Prepare yourself for the possibility of taking a short trip and becoming involved in lots of neighborhood activities. You may change your appearance in some way or give some serious thought to redoing your room. The pace is likely to pick up with your friends and lots of time will be spent hanging out at your house. And if that's not enough, creativity is in your court right now, so think about signing up for an art class!

Taurus

The Bull
April 21–May 20

FAST FACTS ABOUT TAURUS

You love: being recognized for your persistence and patience

Your key colors: green and pink

Your power flowers: pink roses

Your star stones: sapphires and rose quartz

Your metals: copper and brass

Your astro animals: bulls and cows

Your day of the week: Friday

Your ruling planet: Venus, which symbolizes love and beauty

Your motto: I have.

AT YOUR BEST, you're seen as someone who is:

Dependable
Patient
Attentive
Artistic
Resourceful

AT YOUR WORST, you come across as someone who is:

Slow-moving
Insensitive
Stubborn
Prone to procrastinating
Easily embarrassed

YOUR SIGN IS ASSOCIATED WITH:

Prosperity
Harmony
Security
Determination
Cautiousness

YOUR STELLAR STYLE

OK, this is no bull. If you're a typical Taurus, you accept people as they are, are very loyal to your friends, and have lots of common sense. You hate it when things around you

9

seem superficial or fake . . . and that applies to objects as well as people. And you may as well know that as a Taurus, you might very well be one of the most levelheaded, well-adjusted people around. Could be 'cause you're an earth sign, which translates into having a very down-to-earth approach to life. But this doesn't mean you're so stable and rock steady that you're never up for cutting loose. In fact, Taureans are also known for their full-on love for having loads of fun.

WHAT YOU NEED TO SUCCEED

When you're given the option to take your time with whatever it is you're focusing on, you're sure to make your mark. You have an amazing ability to remain very tuned in to what needs to be done. Being left to figure things out for yourself is a much better learning method for you than being hurried and rushed by those around you. Like your sign's symbol, the bull, you are productive and powerful when you're given the chance to set your own pace.

You also crave having fun but you shouldn't become so caught up in the festivities that you lose track of the stuff that's really important. Make sure you devote time to the serious things (like school) that'll help you get ahead down the road. By exhibiting a little more of your serious side and by adding a dash of self-discipline to the scene, you will be on your way to making some of your life-time dreams come true.

FAMILY MATTERS

You're often the first to run to the rescue when things flare up among family members. While it's cool to try to keep the peace, don't let your goodwill-ambassador status prevent you from making yourself heard when some-thing's really annoying you. You are prone to bottling up what's bugging you. This can result in a major out-of-the-blue blowup that throws everyone for a loop. If you speak up when something's rubbing you the wrong way, you're likely to have a much smoother situa-tion at home.

STUDY STYLES THAT SUIT YOUR SIGN

A nose-to-the-grindstone girl, you're pretty serious about your studies. You work hard at your homework and your "slow and steady wins the race" approach to all things aca-demic tends to serve you much better than trying to cram the night before big tests like some of your friends do. Your ultimate study environment is a familiar place where you repeatedly park yourself. A calm and orderly desk at home or a tucked-away table at a library give you the kind of space you need.

WHAT MAKES YOU A SOCIAL STAR

It's your down-to-earth attitude that wins over all your pals. When those supersensitive friends of yours start to freak, you're the one who helps them put things back in perspective. You also have an uncanny ability to make even the most boring events seem special. You may not have a huge circle of friends, but that's because you're pretty selective about who makes the cut. You value friends who are as loyal and dependable as you are, so you prefer to opt for quality over quantity. Among your best pals, your diplomatic nature is put into action when conflict arises and you're put at the helm to calm a crisis and increase the peace.

YOUR HEALTHY ASTRO ATTITUDE

While you're into being active, you may not be all that fast on your feet. Tap into your earthy personality by taking to the trails. Hiking, backpacking, mountain-biking — any activity that puts you in touch with the great outdoors is right for you. You'd also be a natural at playing a defensive position for a soccer, softball, or basketball team. Oh, and when you're in full snack-attack mode, go ahead and give in . . . as long as you burn it off later by doing something sporty.

FUTURE THINK

OK, we don't want to sound too superficial here, but Taureans are totally associated with money and material goods. Since you're born under a sign that's said to be cash savvy, why not look to jobs that concern themselves with currency? Good career investments for you could be jobs in the banking industry or on Wall Street. Doesn't sound like your scene? Other options that make the most of your sign's strengths include jobs that allow you to be heard. Your voice is an asset, so a job as an interviewer, news anchor, or just about any position in the field of broadcasting could be up your alley. Other options worth considering include becoming an artist, sculptor, actor, fashion designer, singer, or real estate agent.

ASTRO ADVICE ALWAYS

Spend some time on your own.

Stay superfocused in order to achieve your goals.

Pair up with a new pal, which could lead to a great opportunity.

Prepare for getting some special recognition at school.

WINNING MOVES
FOR THE MONTHS AHEAD

Open yourself up to learning from the people in your life. While at first their suggestions may seem kind of lame, you may just discover that their advice is actually very grounded and worth following. Also, it may seem like an authority figure is standing in your way but it could be that he or she is just trying to keep you from making a bad decision. If you end up feeling stuck in a rut and are thinking about busting out of it by doing something risky, don't! It'll only lead to you having to talk your way out of a situation at home. To avoid upsetting things on the home front, focus on schoolwork and future plans instead.

Gemini

The Twins
May 21–June 20

FAST FACTS ABOUT GEMINI

You love: mental challenges and interesting discussions

Your key colors: all shades of yellow

Your power flowers: bright yellow daffodils

Your star stones: yellow diamonds and citrine

Your metal: quicksilver

Your astro animals: deer and rabbits

Your day of the week: Wednesday

Your ruling planet: Mercury, which symbolizes youth, relationships, and change

Your motto: I think.

AT YOUR BEST, you're seen as someone who is:

Inquisitive
Inventive
Entertaining
Versatile
Open-minded

AT YOUR WORST, you come across as someone who is:

Restless
Easily bored
Impatient
Gossipy
A split personality

YOUR SIGN IS ASSOCIATED WITH:

Communication
Persuasion
Curiosity
Learning
Adaptability

YOUR STELLAR STYLE

While you have a natural love for learning and tend to focus on stuff that's cerebral, the fact that your sign's symbol is the twins means you are dually influenced by your heart and your head. You tend to gravitate toward things in life that touch you emotionally *and* intellectually. Born under the sign of the twins, you may be secretly in search of your soul mate, someone who you feel completes you. You're a composite of many different personality traits and sometimes you confuse even the people who know you best. Don't be surprised if they say, "Will the real you please stand up?"

WHAT YOU NEED TO SUCCEED

Inventive and original, you like to be given the opportunity to originate ideas and implement new ways to solve problems. Because you're superadaptable, you're the one who can make the most of situations that others may find disagreeable or see as major setbacks. You are also versatile and capable of enjoying and excelling at many different things. Just don't let yourself get pulled in too many directions or you'll end up becoming scattered and distracted. Figure out a course of action and stick to it.

FAMILY MATTERS

If there's one thing your family can count on from you, it's conversation. You are the girl with the gift of gab. Just be on the alert for going a bit too far with what you blurt out. Tempting though it may be to gossip and spread the news, you can get burned big-time if you become known for being the family tattletale. When conversations turn confidential, keep what's told to you under lock and key.

STUDY STYLES THAT SUIT YOUR SIGN
OK, you're kind of a clock-watcher. The thing is, when a subject bores you beyond belief, you're not the kind of girl who can hide the way you're feeling. You are a quick study but since restless is your middle name, a subject has got to be riveting to hold your attention. While in class, be careful not to spend all your time staring out the window or whispering to friends. Any subjects that let you showcase your conversational skills are the ones you're apt to ace. Think foreign languages and language arts. If there's a speech and debate club at your school, sign up.

WHAT MAKES YOU A SOCIAL STAR
As a supersocial Gemini, you are amusing, entertaining, witty, and can have four conversations at once without missing a beat. You

shine socially when you're around others who are talkative and into what's supercurrent. People who report on yesterday's news cause you to yawn. And drama queens are the last people on earth with whom you're likely to hang — they wear you out in a big way. You prefer to spend time with people who are able to maintain an even keel. You enjoy paying lots of attention to your closest friends and have no problem doing what you can to make them look good. But be aware that you have a tendency to flit from one thing or person to another and that this could end up causing your buds to occasionally see you as a flake of a friend.

YOUR HEALTHY ASTRO ATTITUDE

Focus on those activities that enable you to move your arms around. Create a racket with tennis, squash, or badminton. The net result of these games, in addition to giving you a great workout, is that they allow you to show off your grace and form. The movement and choreography of all varieties of dance make for great stay-in-shape choices. And remember, any workout is more fun when you do it with friends, so enlist a bunch of your buds to get buff with you.

FUTURE THINK

Great jobs for Geminis include anything that lets you talk your way to the top. Consider careers in broadcasting, radio, or public speaking. Given your gift of gab, you'd also be a great salesperson or spokesperson for a major corporation. Think talk's cheap? Hardly. With you, it can be the way to complete career success. Other options include becoming a writer, teacher, journalist, lecturer, or linguist.

ASTRO ADVICE ALWAYS

Compromise with a family member and come up with a smart solution.
Pay attention to your intuition when making a major decision.
Be a team player in one of your classes.
Keep communication open with your best friend.

WINNING MOVES
FOR THE MONTHS AHEAD

You're going to be running around with lots of nervous energy. Work this to your advantage by enrolling in an exercise class and getting in top shape. If something should come to an end, as in a relationship that's historically been pretty rocky, give yourself time to think about what it meant to you and then move on. You'll be building yourself a better future by not dwelling on what went wrong. Focus on what may lie ahead. While events may leave you feeling as if you're emotionally scattered and scurrying about in an aimless way, honing in on a few of your goals and figuring out what it will take to achieve them will help adjust your attitude.

Cancer

The Crab
June 21–July 20

FAST FACTS ABOUT CANCER

You love: being seen as dependable and protective by your friends

Your key colors: white, silver, and pearly shades of gray

Your power flowers: white roses

Your star stones: pearls and moonstones

Your metals: silver and aluminum

Your astro animals: crabs and other crustaceans

Your day of the week: Monday

Your ruling planet: the moon, which symbolizes intuition and memory

Your motto: I feel.

AT YOUR BEST, you're seen as someone who is:

Compassionate
Helpful
Caring
Protective
Sensitive of others

AT YOUR WORST, you come across as someone who is:

Possessive
Easily hurt
Moody
Stuck in their ways
Selfish

YOUR SIGN IS ASSOCIATED WITH:

Sensitivity
Comfort
Nostalgia
History
Security

YOUR STELLAR STYLE

You're all about compassion. You're first on the scene to help out a friend or to crusade for a cause that's important to you. Sensitive and naturally tuned in to the feelings of others, you're almost psychic in your ability to draw out your friends. Your first impressions about people are rarely wrong. The flip side of your personality? Well, since your sign's symbol is the crab, when your mood switches gears you can come across as the Countess of Crabdom. You have a tendency to withdraw into your own little world rather than stage a major outburst or create a big scene. But don't think you're fooling anyone with your slow-brewing method. When you get steamed and finally do blow your top, people definitely feel the heat!

WHAT YOU NEED TO SUCCEED

You operate best when you feel secure in your surroundings. You like tangible proof and have an "I need to see it to believe it" attitude. You relish receiving tons of nurturing from those you're close to. When you feel depleted, turn to your loved ones for a quick hug or a personalized pep talk. Because you are so supersensitive, you have the tendency to read too much into situations, jump to the wrong conclusion, get hurt, and then retreat into your protective shell. Trying to put things into perspective might help you better achieve your goals.

FAMILY MATTERS

Don't retreat into that shell of yours. Those who care about you want to hear what you think. Trust 'em enough to open up and share your feelings. It's totally possible to have a healthier environment on the home front but it'll call for a little more honesty and openness on your part.

STUDY STYLES THAT SUIT YOUR SIGN

You do best in subjects in which you're allowed to showcase your natural creativity. Any subject that allows you to write short stories or poetry or otherwise express yourself is right up your alley. Also, think about packing plenty of art and music classes into your schedule. Pay attention to the basics covered in all your school subjects and, if given the choice, always go with an original way of completing an assignment. Cancers are often the ones who discover new and interesting ways to solve problems. Believe in yourself and don't be afraid to let your vivid imagination help you slide into your rightful position on the honor roll.

WHAT MAKES YOU A SOCIAL STAR

You have an amazing ability to draw out other people even though you yourself are prone to retreating. You've been known to wait for others to introduce themselves to you instead of making the first move, but once the hellos are out of the way, you're apt to be a forever kind of friend. You're at your social best and are really able to shine when hanging with the people you trust most.

YOUR HEALTHY ASTRO ATTITUDE
Could be 'cause you're a crab, but water sports really work for you. Whether you stick with the steady rhythm of swimming laps or go for the adventure of waterskiing, you should try to tap into all the advantages of being part of the wet set. On the food front, watch out for overindulging on fat-free treats. The fat may be missing but the sugar and calories can still add up to a snacking style that doesn't make sense. Chow down on some fresh fruit instead.

FUTURE THINK
You've got a natural love for all things nostalgic. Why not have a blast with the past by considering a career as a museum curator, an antique dealer, or a historian? Directing film documentaries or becoming a fashion or studio photographer are also options that will

allow you to take your own place in history. Also, look to jobs that'll let you tap into your nurturing nature, such as being a doctor, nurse, or social worker. To key into the more creative side of your personality, consider a career as an interior designer or an architect.

ASTRO ADVICE ALWAYS

Put extra energy into your schoolwork and it will pay off for you.
Tune into what others are trying to tell you.
Remain patient and stay practical if you want a certain situation to play in your favor.
Turn to your family and friends for support.

WINNING MOVES
FOR THE MONTHS AHEAD

You've been faced with lots of challenges lately. And since you're supersensitive, it's been extra important for you to know that your friends are there for you. You may feel that someone close to you has let you down in a major way. But rather than obsessing over it, let go of your anger. While a friend may have disappointed you, you should spend some time learning to trust your instincts about people and take the chance at making some new friends.

27

Leo
The Lion
July 21–August 21

FAST FACTS ABOUT LEO

You love: people seeing you as someone with a love of life and an ability to organize and lead

Your key colors: regal shades such as red, purple, and gold

Your power flowers: marigolds, sunflowers, and tiger lilies

Your star stones: peridot and amber

Your metal: gold

Your astro animals: lions, tigers, and all the big cats

Your day of the week: Sunday

Your ruling planet: the sun (though it's really a star), which symbolizes life, exploration, and authority

Your motto: I will.

AT YOUR BEST, you're seen as someone who is:

Loyal
Dignified
Kind
Generous
Courageous

AT YOUR WORST, you come across as someone who is:

Stubborn
Arrogant
Smug
Prone to bragging
Sometimes sulky

YOUR SIGN IS ASSOCIATED WITH:

Entertainment
Recognition
Performance
Drama
Hospitality

YOUR STELLAR STYLE

Like the regal lion that's the symbol of your sign, you love to be the center of attention. You strive to be the best at everything you undertake. Ruled by the sun, it's no big surprise that you love to shine. To make the most of your royal disposition, you make a point of maintaining a sunny personality and take pride in your accomplishments. You're seen as someone who's very personable and friendly.

WHAT YOU NEED TO SUCCEED

Attention, applause, compliments, spotlights, and standing ovations. You get the idea. To truly shine, you need top billing. After all, you're the top cat. Surround yourself with people who will supply you with plenty of praise. Also, you definitely do have a lion's share of things to be proud about, but bail on bragging. This doesn't mean you have to hide in the background. Others want to see you succeed, but compromise is key. Just allow others their time in the sun as well.

FAMILY MATTERS

Everyone under your roof needs some time to feel like a star. Try to avoid upstaging the rest of your family members and there will be more harmony at home. If you want to hear praise from your parents, consider throwing some compliments their way, too. And rather than always behaving in a way that puts you first, practice sharing more with your siblings and offer to back them up when they need extra support.

STUDY STYLES THAT SUIT YOUR SIGN
Chances are, your impulsive nature has caused you not to bust open those books as often as you should. Rather than looking at all those assignments as a cage trapping you in your room, treat even that way-dry subject matter as new territory to explore. That king-of-the-jungle interest in exploration and staking out new turf can really take you places if you apply it to learning and homework assignments. Because of your proud nature, you are likely to rebel against someone telling you what to do — you much prefer being asked.

WHAT MAKES YOU A SOCIAL STAR
It's pretty easy for you to make new friends because you're very likely to have an outgoing and open personality. You have a need to be liked, so you love to be part of a big group. When you plunk yourself into the middle of the largest gathering of people at a party, within just a few minutes the whole focus of the conversation often turns to the topic you've introduced. While this is a trait that many admire, don't abuse it. Most people

31

want to actively participate in conversations rather than just be a member of the audience. Also, be sure to socialize in a way that won't appear to others as though you always have to be the star.

YOUR HEALTHY ASTRO ATTITUDE

Choose workouts that also allow for socializing: tennis, dancing — even a couple of rounds of bowling! Schedule lots of short walks into your routine. It's a great way to burn off calories and some of that nervous energy you tend to carry around. Like the caged lion, if you're not given the chance to roam, you're prone to anxious pacing! You should also stand tall and proud by paying close attention to your posture. Your competitive nature means you always play to win.

FUTURE THINK

Sign up for a future that allows you to take center stage. If it's not you yourself in the spotlight, then you're likely at least to want what you've created to be on display. Just about any job in the entertainment field would allow you to shine. Also, think about becoming an artist, athlete, executive, or government official.

ASTRO ADVICE ALWAYS
Stay calm even though one of your oldest friendships may feel threatened.
Listen to what an adult you trust has to say.
Focus on your studies.
Be loyal to an old friend and she'll be there for you when you need her most.

WINNING MOVES
FOR THE MONTHS AHEAD
A phone call could bring amazing news your way. Plan to spend extra time with a sibling or other relative to help him or her through a rough situation. Also plan on spending more time than usual on your own. It may feel kind of uncomfortable at first since you're such a social animal, but after your participation in loads of action-packed events, you'll need to recharge your batteries. Listen to calming music and take plenty of "cat" naps.

Virgo

The Virgin or Maiden
August 22–September 22

FAST FACTS ABOUT VIRGO

You love: being seen as someone who is perceptive and patient

Your key colors: blues and greens

Your power flowers: forget-me-nots

Your star stones: emeralds and clear quartz

Your metal: quicksilver

Your astro animals: brown bears and squirrels

Your day of the week: Wednesday

Your ruling planets: Mercury, which symbolizes adaptability and diplomacy

Your motto: I analyze.

AT YOUR BEST, you're seen as someone who is:
Gentle
Helpful
Organized
Dedicated
Witty

AT YOUR WORST, you come across as someone who is:
Prone to worrying
Prudish
Undemonstrative
Overly demanding of others
Prone to irritability

YOUR SIGN IS ASSOCIATED WITH:
Honesty
Character
Modesty
Health
Reliability

YOUR STELLAR STYLE
You are very tuned into your senses and can be a bit too hard on yourself. Lighten up and realize that you are viewed by others as one

35

of the most warm-hearted, kind, and responsible people around. As a Virgo, you are likely to be graceful and dignified and don't get any thrill from drawing attention to yourself. Your keen perception and sharp eye means you are often the first person to notice mistakes and flaws — watch out you don't alienate friends with hypercritical remarks.

WHAT YOU NEED TO SUCCEED

An orderly, calm environment keeps you content. When things get chaotic and there doesn't seem to be anyone in charge, you've been known to panic. Loud noise and too many things going on at once really rattle your nerves. To do your best, stake out a serene scene. While you may be tempted to hang in the background, force your way to the front occasionally. You'll be amazed at the way it makes you feel. That kinda-quiet-keeps-to-herself girl will transform into someone who comes across as completely confident. Give it a shot. When you want to resume being your usual demure self, have no fear. Your unassuming nature will easily kick right back into gear.

Consider getting rid of the things in your

life that are no longer useful. Lots of clutter doesn't allow for the "space" you need for new things to come into your world. Plus, organizing your stuff and getting your thoughts in order will lead to a more organized life.

FAMILY MATTERS

Being a do-good daughter is one thing. Becoming the family doormat is another. Wipe away that welcome-mat mentality. Also, recognize that you are more sensitive than most to teasing and being the subject of pranks. Lighten up and let the levity of a relative's mood rub off on you.

STUDY STYLES THAT SUIT YOUR SIGN

Because you love to learn and are a hard worker, most subjects (especially the practical ones) are easy for you to ace. You're the one whose work is always put up on the wall. Tap into some of your best memories of being a little kid and odds are some of 'em will center around magical places, fairy tales, and amazing myths. Now that you've outgrown your OshKosh overalls, consider taking classes that let you be creative and remind you of what being a little kid was all about.

WHAT MAKES YOU A SOCIAL STAR

When it comes to making friends, you're kind of choosy. Your feeling is that it's better to have a few true-blue friends than a whole swarm of casual acquaintances. You're especially into friends who have a sense of direction to their lives. Slackers put you off. And any form of indecisiveness drives you absolutely up the wall.

YOUR HEALTHY ASTRO ATTITUDE

Naturally disciplined, you have what it takes to stick with a strict workout regimen. Tap into the things that matter most to you in order to come up with a shape-up strategy you're likely to stick with. For instance, since people born under your sign are known for being kind of vain, work with it. Use it as a strategy for focusing on staying fit! By being physically fit, you'll look and feel better. Challenge yourself to try out a new sport.

FUTURE THINK

Your respect for organization and order makes jobs in the criminal justice system or the legal field good choices. Because of your uncanny ability to find logical solutions to problems and because of your perfectionist nature, you'd also make a great doctor, psychiatrist, or scientist. Other made-for-order occupations for those born under your sign are those of accountant, teacher, veterinarian, and librarian.

ASTRO ADVICE ALWAYS
Drop an old habit and make a positive change.
Look to the little things to make you happy.
Tap into your creative juices.
Take on added responsibility.

WINNING MOVES
FOR THE MONTHS AHEAD
Your fairly predictable schedule may undergo a shake-up of some sort. No need to panic, though. The change could bring about some serious excitement. Stay open to the idea of making changes in your plans and it will help you adjust to the many new opportunities that are about to enter your life. Some type of field trip or educational opportunity is likely to have a big influence on your future studies.

Libra

The Scales
September 23–October 22

FAST FACTS ABOUT LIBRA

You love: elegance and all things romantic
Your key colors: light blue and shades of pink
Your power flowers: violets
Your star stones: sapphires and blue topaz
Your metals: copper and brass
Your astro animals: elephants and rhinos
Your day of the week: Friday
Your ruling planet: Venus, which symbolizes justice and love of the arts
Your motto: I balance.

AT YOUR BEST, you're seen as someone who is:
Artistic
A great negotiator
Romantic
Fair-minded
Sincere

AT YOUR WORST, you come across as someone who is:
Sulky
Indecisive
Flirtatious
Fearful
Manipulative

YOUR SIGN IS ASSOCIATED WITH:
Relationships
Diplomacy
Balance
Sophistication
Refinement

YOUR STELLAR STYLE
You stay fine-tuned to the whereabouts of all the important people in your life. In fact, it could even be you're a little scared to spend time solo. Though you radiate calm, cool, and

collected vibes, your knees might be knocking together at the thought of being left alone. Pay attention to the Libra symbol of the scales. Scales are about balance. By striving for a well-adjusted balance between social and solo time, you'll come across as someone who's an excellent partner or member of a team but also able to fly fearlessly when required to go it alone. It's important to schedule time to be on your own. And when you are with others, let them get to know you better by not hiding your true feelings. Speak up and give everyone a chance to get to know the real you.

WHAT YOU NEED TO SUCCEED

You like to feel that you're part of the team. Acceptance is very important to you. As one who wants to do well and appear diplomatic, you need to hang out in harmonious environments among people who play fair. Affection and attention matter to you, so keep company with a cool crowd. They'll help you learn to be yourself. As a Libran, your desire for harmony is so strong that you risk becoming a total people pleaser. To get ahead, try to do some things for yourself instead of always trying to please others. Stick to your decisions.

FAMILY MATTERS

You love your family but there's no need to cling to them like Saran Wrap. Develop friendships and some outside interests so that you're not left feeling all alone when family members have other plans. You're so sweet and sentimental, there's simply no way for your family *not* to know how much you care about 'em.

STUDY STYLES THAT SUIT YOUR SIGN

While this may sound weird, you actually thrive in an academic environment where you're given instructions and told what to do. You absorb information from all sources, especially books, and rarely need to be told to study. You excel at anything creative — music, art, poetry, or drama. Your strong sense of responsibility guides you toward getting those great grades.

WHAT MAKES YOU A SOCIAL STAR

You're very considerate and appreciative of people's differences but you have a very low tolerance for folks who are irresponsible. You're generous toward the friends who matter most to you and are usually the one who loves to be in charge of staging big birthday celebrations, putting together sentimental scrapbooks, and recognizing special events. Conflict makes you crazy, so you are an expert at smoothing ruffled feathers. But be careful not to just appease people by telling them what they want to hear.

YOUR HEALTHY ASTRO ATTITUDE

Exercise is not exactly something that excites you. Your best bet is to schedule miniworkouts so the thought of gearing up for exercise won't seem quite so overwhelming. A couple laps in a pool or a walk around the block will motivate you to keep up the pace. Or sign up for a fun class with a friend and start thinking of your workouts as social situations. And if a workout is really gonna make you sweat, you say, "Yuck!" So think about scheduling activities that invigorate you without leaving you perspiring too heavily. And when it comes to satisfying that sweet tooth, go with naturally yummy treats like strawberries, peaches, and fruit smoothies.

FUTURE THINK

Point yourself toward a career path that'll take you to creative places where polite people surround you. Emotionally charged environments are not where you want to be. Consider a career — interior design, architecture, museum curator — that blends both your natural artistic and business skills. Your knack for diplomacy would make a career as a lawyer, judge, counselor, or diplomat a great choice. To showcase your more creative side, consider becoming a decorator, musician, or artist.

ASTRO ADVICE ALWAYS

Pay attention! Unexpected events will lead to some amazing opportunities.

Prepare for challenges in your life that will bring great rewards.

Expect travel to show you a new way of doing things.

Plan to be more active than ever.

WINNING MOVES
FOR THE MONTHS AHEAD

Your creative ideas will take you places. People in your life are likely to comment on your inspirational ideas. A social situation that could result in an embarrassing glitch will actually give you the opportunity to meet someone you've always wanted to get to know. Be on the alert for friends who will offer you help in making a critical decision about your future.

45

Scorpio

The Scorpion
October 23–November 22

FAST FACTS ABOUT SCORPIO

You love: being seen as someone who is strong enough to rally after setbacks

Your key colors: red and black

Your power flowers: gardenias and orchids

Your star stones: jasper and clear quartz

Your metals: plutonium and steel

Your astro animals: wolves and coyotes

Your day of the week: Tuesday

Your ruling planet: Pluto, which symbolizes rebirth and transformation

Your motto: I desire.

AT YOUR BEST, you're seen as someone who is:
Passionate
Protective
Concerned
Investigative
Not easily shocked

AT YOUR WORST, you come across as someone who is:
Possessive
Jealous
Insulting
Cunning
Quick-tempered

YOUR SIGN IS ASSOCIATED WITH:
Transformation
Change
Secrets
Discovery
Defense

YOUR STELLAR STYLE
Ruled by Pluto, Scorpios come across as completely cool with their surroundings. The truth is, that poised performance is often just that — a bit of an act. See, as a Scorp you're

actually a secretive soul. You're slow to reveal who you really are to others. And just when people are pretty sure they've got you figured out, you completely transform yourself. This can be a creative force in your life or one that's kind of destructive. Some people will see your love of change as exciting but others may think you're just trying to win them over and will see you as superficial. Rather than reinventing yourself at such a rapid rate, consider allowing some people you trust to get to know the real you.

WHAT YOU NEED TO SUCCEED

Superresourceful, you continue to excel long after others have given up. You need to be allowed to fight your own battles. You have strong willpower and when you set your mind to achieving a particular task, you often are able to pull it off with ease. You're very capable and thrive under pressure. When most of your friends are ready to give up, you're the one who wants to give it one more chance. But you also have an impatient nature, so you need to remember not to sweat the small stuff. Save your energy for the things that matter most.

FAMILY MATTERS

When you're in doubt about how a member of your family is feeling, it's best to ask. You have a tendency to be a bit too impulsive and have been known to assume the worst about others' completely innocent behavior. To control this far-from-trustworthy tendency, ask others to explain their actions and their feelings. Strive to keep a lid on emotional outbursts.

STUDY STYLES THAT SUIT YOUR SIGN

In a classroom setting you've got to be challenged. You hate when teachers hover over you while you work on assignments in class. You need your space and are quick to react to criticism. While you can get your homework done in just about any environment (yes, even with that CD player blaring at Warp 9), you really only feel you're succeeding when someone serves up some praise about your academic achievements.

WHAT MAKES YOU A SOCIAL STAR

You are not one who can be described as wishy-washy. First impressions matter to you and your gut reaction upon meeting someone new tends to be amazingly accurate. You've even been known to freak out your friends with some of your right-on-the-money readings of people. Others find you exciting and fascinating, so it's a sure bet you have many admirers — just try not to scare them all away by coming on too strong.

YOUR HEALTHY ASTRO ATTITUDE

To stay in shape, set specific goals and consider working out every day. You have tons of energy and thrive on adrenaline rushes, but it's best to burn off some of that excess energy with regular daily workouts. Tap into your sign's sense of determination by forcing yourself to get more psyched about fitness. Load up on lots of fresh, natural foods and focus on figuring out which sports are the ones you're most likely to stick with. Once you find an activity that's right for you, your body will get in gear.

FUTURE THINK

Ever considered a career in the public arena? Think about it. Though you work well on your own, you should look for a job that allows you to share your knowledge with others. You'll want to be an expert in your field, whatever it is you choose. Your love of mystery makes detective work, military intelligence, politics, or medicine great options. Also, a job that has an element of unearthing clues or discovering things, such as being an archaeologist or a pathologist, fits you to a T.

ASTRO ADVICE ALWAYS
Get to know more about one of your friends — she may be going through a tough time at home.
Take on a challenging task.
Prepare for some unexpected cash to come your way.
Let an older relative know that he or she is loved.

WINNING MOVES
FOR THE MONTHS AHEAD
You'll be in the mood to sit down with one of your best friends and make some major plans about how to spend your next vacation. You are going to gain new confidence in yourself and will try something you never thought you'd be up for. Keep all areas of your life balanced and stable. Lots of sudden changes could prove to be chaotic.

Sagittarius

The Archer or the Centaur
November 23–December 20

FAST FACTS ABOUT SAGITTARIUS

You love: being seen as someone who is optimistic and honest

Your key colors: deep purples and blues

Your power flowers: carnations

Your star stones: turquoise and lapis lazuli

Your metal: tin

Your astro animals: horses and dogs

Your day of the week: Thursday

Your ruling planet: Jupiter, which symbolizes justice and fairness and encourages constant learning

Your motto: I understand.

AT YOUR BEST, you're seen as someone who is:
Optimistic
Honest
Enthusiastic
Inspiring
Open to what others have to say

AT YOUR WORST, you come across as someone who is:
Argumentative
Impatient
Indulgent
A risk taker
Not prone to planning ahead

YOUR SIGN IS ASSOCIATED WITH:
Idealism
Travel
Justice
Intellect
Generosity

YOUR STELLAR STYLE
Like the centaur, your sign's symbol, others perceive you as someone who is prepared, eager for adventure, and always on the move. A restless spirit, you are constantly pursuing

53

your dreams and are bothered by things in life that seem to hold you back from achieving them. An idealistic girl by nature, you picture your future in a positive way and you can't wait to get there! Parties and social events are made for you. You bring tons of fun into the lives of lots of people and are quick to turn others on to the possibilities life has to offer. Your ability to get others to broaden their take on what they can accomplish in life is a skill that everyone around you admires.

You're bold, adventurous, and enjoy spending time with people who share your love of life. Your sense of humor helps diffuse tension among your friends. Your honesty makes you a good friend but sometimes you can be too up-front for your own good — this bluntness can deal up some serious blows.

WHAT YOU NEED TO SUCCEED
To really excel, you need an environment where you don't feel pressured. When you feel as if you're under the watchful eye of a teacher or parent, you're inclined to withdraw from your studies. You benefit from guidelines and schedules that are spelled out because, left on your own, you tend to put off everything until the last minute and then have

to work like crazy to get it all done. You need some rules but you can't handle feeling tied down. Wait for all conditions to be just right before going after what you want. Hard work will pay off for you and bring lots of good fortune in the future.

FAMILY MATTERS

When things get tense under your family's roof, your sense of humor has been known to save the day. Just don't put your sarcasm into overdrive. You have a natural rapport with people from all age groups, so whether you're trying to calm down the cousin who's having a "terrible twos" attack or listening to the grandma who gabs too much, you're the one the family is always happy to have around. But when it's your turn to do chores around the house, you're often quick to flee the scene. Try to help out a bit more. It could work to your advantage in the future.

STUDY STYLES THAT SUIT YOUR SIGN

People often make comments about where you choose to situate yourself for studying, but the reality is that you concentrate best when your surroundings are comfortable and offer plenty of fresh air. Confining classrooms can really get to you. But be careful of your tendency to stare out windows wishing you weren't stuck in school or you might end up missing a big test announcement. When a field trip appears on the schedule of events, you're the first to sign up. Exploring the world around you is one of the ways you tap into your creativity. Think about signing up for a geography or world history class. That way, on the days when you've gotta stay put, you can at least pretend you're pulling out a passport!

WHAT MAKES YOU A SOCIAL STAR

You have a love of life that's completely contagious. You're likely to have a large circle of friends. If life were spent on an ocean liner, you'd be the cruise director. Supersocial, you love to set up spur-of-the-moment activities. But if anyone dares to act possessive toward you, watch out! You are likely to give 'em the old heave-ho! You hate to feel "owned" by anyone and will shake off friends who seem too clingy. Your need to feel free and unencumbered on the social scene makes it easy for you to get along with just about everyone. You are usually up for practically anything social and have a hard time saying no.

YOUR HEALTHY ASTRO ATTITUDE

Team sports are where it's at for those born under your sign. Work some weight training into your routine between those group practices. You have a daring, adventurous streak and are just the kind of girl to sign up for a mountain trek or a downhill skiing event. Any sport that involves exploration, such as hiking, backpacking, cross-country skiing, or mountain biking, satisfies your wandering ways. Splurge on some sporty new workout sneakers and then strap 'em on! Ditch the indoor workouts and gear up for the great outdoors.

FUTURE THINK

You are fun-loving, laid-back, and need your freedom, so look for a job that'll let you try new things. Sign up with a company that allows for plenty of advancement or opportunities to travel. You'd make a great travel agent, salesperson, entrepreneur, or professional athlete. Think about being an interpreter, foreign correspondent, or ambassador. Other options include becoming a publisher, judge, teacher, member of the clergy, or publicist.

ASTRO ADVICE ALWAYS

Tap into your emotions to find the answer to a problem that's been bugging you.

Get ready to receive lots of attention and praise.

Keep a lid on your spending style.

Give a friend a needed blast of confidence.

WINNING MOVES
FOR THE MONTHS AHEAD

You may have to put in way more work than you anticipated in one of your favorite school subjects. Hang in there, though, because the results will be rewarding. Something will happen socially that'll allow you to shine. You will be given lots of opportunities to work hard and impress just about everyone!

Capricorn

The Mountain Goat
December 21–January 19

FAST FACTS ABOUT CAPRICORN

You love: putting in whatever it takes to succeed at everything you try

Your key colors: steely gray and forest green

Your power flowers: poppies

Your star stones: lapis lazuli and smoky quartz

Your metal: lead

Your astro animals: goats and reindeer

Your day of the week: Saturday

Your ruling planet: Saturn, which symbolizes ambition and persistence

Your motto: I use.

AT YOUR BEST, you're seen as someone who is:
Organized
Hardworking
Ambitious
Concerned
Respectful of authority

AT YOUR WORST, you come across as someone who is:
Critical
Miserly
Anxious
Controlling
A perfectionist

YOUR SIGN IS ASSOCIATED WITH:
Accomplishment
Determination
Persistence
Discipline
Success

YOUR STELLAR STYLE
Ruled by Saturn, you tend to be serious and hardworking. In fact, you're seen as one of the most diligent and determined members of the zodiac. You might think others see you as someone who's kind of boring, but the truth is

that most people wish they could be more like you. Your persistence and pragmatic approach to challenges means you're often the one who's worked her way to the top of the summit before anyone else has even begun to make the climb.

WHAT YOU NEED TO SUCCEED

Challenges that allow you to strive to set new goals for yourself bring out the best in you. You are instilled with a strong sense of duty and are able to set your own rules and goals. A well-organized study area is as important for your academic success as is peace and quiet — you can't deal with noise and crowds. You need to work on balancing your life between work and play. Stick to your goals even if it seems like you're up against an awful lot of obstacles. But also be sure to allow your serious side to fall by the wayside on occasion by making some time for fun.

FAMILY MATTERS

Your love of being in charge can cause you to order others around. Rather than barking at your sibs as if you're a drill sergeant, consider asking them for their opinions. Because you can be quite the boss, you'll get along much better with your sibs if you refrain from issuing orders and listen to their ideas for once.

STUDY STYLES THAT SUIT YOUR SIGN

You do well in just about every subject. Good grades don't always come easily for you but you work hard to make sure you get them. While most of your classmates dread walking through those school doors, you secretly celebrate when school starts. It's not that you're an academia addict, it's just that school is a place that allows you to showcase your dedicated and disciplined nature.

WHAT MAKES YOU A SOCIAL STAR

You gain the trust of others because you're seen as someone who is polite and reliable. It's very rare for you to turn your back on a friend who's in trouble. Your steadfast style and loyalty translate into friendships that can last a lifetime.

YOUR HEALTHY ASTRO ATTITUDE

Moderation is key. A repetitious routine is cool by you, but avoid pushing yourself too hard. Being too rigid and sapping your energy can lead to sports injuries. Be happy with moderate, steady results from your workouts rather than going for a dramatic transformation. Like the mountain goat, you show signs of rugged individualism. Singles tennis or running in track events in which you're on your own are the best ways for you to achieve your personal best. Keep track of your workout results by logging them in a fitness journal. You'll see signs of improvement right away.

FUTURE THINK

Your natural good taste and great judgment make you an ideal candidate for any executive office! Given your sign's strengths, you might consider a career in government, science, or environmental politics. You have extremely high standards, solid beliefs, and traditional values. A career as a banker, systems analyst, researcher, engineer, politician, manager, real estate broker, architect, or government official would be a good match for your methodical style.

ASTRO ADVICE ALWAYS

Accept academic challenges.
Focus on breaking that bad habit.
Burst through any negative thinking that's holding you back from trying your best.
Pay attention to authority figures.

WINNING MOVES
FOR THE MONTHS AHEAD

A visit from someone special may disrupt your social schedule but you'll benefit from it in a big way. Present yourself as friendly and approachable and something important could come your way at school. Just don't spread yourself too thin. Since it's important to you to give everything you undertake your absolute all, be careful not to overextend yourself because it could lead to catastrophe.

Aquarius

The Water Bearer
January 20–February 18

FAST FACTS ABOUT AQUARIUS

You love: dreaming about the future and being seen as independent

Your key colors: indigo blue and purple

Your power flowers: lavender and white lilacs

Your star stones: amethysts and aquamarines

Your metal: uranium

Your astro animals: peacocks and hawks

Your day of the week: Saturday

Your ruling planet: Uranus, symbolizing knowledge, invention, and humanitarianism

Your motto: I know.

AT YOUR BEST, you're seen as someone who is:
Thoughtful
Humane
Loyal
Inventive
Independent

AT YOUR WORST, you come across as someone who is:
Self-centered
Lacking in confidence
Overly curious about others
Lacking tact
Unwilling to stick up for beliefs

YOUR SIGN IS ASSOCIATED WITH:
Originality
Independence
Eccentricity
Technology
Humanitarianism

YOUR STELLAR STYLE
Influenced by Uranus, you're seen by others as someone who is unique and totally unpredictable. You're a free spirit who doesn't set out to shock anyone but always seems to do

so because of your outrageous and sometimes way, way out-there ways. You're very independent and have a superstrong need for freedom. While some of your friends are thinking it might be kinda cool to have a boyfriend, you look at the whole coupledom thing as a form of confinement. You're the social activist of the zodiac. Injustice and intolerance are things you just can't understand. While plenty of people will tell you you can't change the world, you're the girl who's gonna try to prove 'em wrong.

WHAT YOU NEED TO SUCCEED

You thrive in an environment where you can be inventive and forward-thinking. While some people may think you are a bit of a flake, you know that lots of your ideas will be admired in the future. When you're allowed to voice your "weird" ideas and act on them, that's when people will really be able to see how innovative and involved you can become in things that interest you.

FAMILY MATTERS

Open up, already! You know that your family means the world to you. But guess what? You

67

don't always let others in on how you feel. A kind of kooky Aquarian trait is that you may give more attention to complete strangers than you do to those people close to you. Here are some tips: Let your dad know you love him. Give your mom a kiss. Hug your sister. Go ahead. It won't hurt.

STUDY STYLES THAT SUIT YOUR SIGN
Since you tend to think about the future, your studies can really take off if you're able to work with new computer programs or do the majority of your research by surfing the Internet. Sign up for whatever computer classes you can and try to log on to some of the newest ways of learning. Since you're a free spirit, you'd probably prefer a progressive type of school over a traditional one.

WHAT MAKES YOU A SOCIAL STAR
You are the humanitarian of the zodiac. You can get along with just about everybody. You are completely against cliques because they just end up making it harder to meet all different kinds of people. Your universal appeal means that there are probably tons of people who consider you a friend.

YOUR HEALTHY ASTRO ATTITUDE

You hate routine but it's actually the best way for you to achieve long-term fitness. Regular workouts (and weigh-ins) allow you to see the results of your efforts. If you're losing your enthusiasm for exercise, consider joining an aerobics class or becoming part of a sports team. Meeting up with others on a regular basis will force you to rally. Also, make room in your schedule to relax. A short nap can leave you with loads more energy.

FUTURE THINK

You're not one to rely on old rules. According to you, outdated ways of doing things should definitely be updated. Your forward-thinking mind is always on the alert to discover the next best thing. Think about a job as a social worker, writer, humanitarian spokesperson, or director of a nonprofit organization. Other ideal occupations include becoming a psychologist, a computer specialist, or an inventor.

ASTRO ADVICE ALWAYS

Free yourself from friends who are negative influences.
Be ready to take advantage of lucky opportunities when they come your way.

Think through your goals and reevaluate 'em if necessary.

Tap into your creativity by writing in a journal on a regular basis.

WINNING MOVES
FOR THE MONTHS AHEAD

An adult at school is going to do his or her best to make you shine in a certain subject. Be open to the ideas that come your way. You'll have lots of fun with one of your best friends but you may need to talk to her about something fairly important so she'll be able to get a true sense of where you stand.

Pisces

The Fish
February 19–March 20

FAST FACTS ABOUT PISCES

You love: being seen as easygoing and super-creative

Your key colors: turquoise and blue-greens

Your power flowers: water lilies and lotus flowers

Your star stones: opals and turquoise

Your metal: platinum

Your astro animals: fish and dolphins

Your day of the week: Thursday

Your ruling planet: Neptune, which symbolizes solitude and mysticism

Your motto: I believe.

AT YOUR BEST, you're seen as someone who is:
Trusting
Helpful
Creative
Gentle
Understanding

AT YOUR WORST, you come across as someone who is:
Self-pitying
Dependent
Insecure
Often putting blame on yourself
Gullible

YOUR SIGN IS ASSOCIATED WITH:
Altruism
Intuition
Sensitivity
Sympathy
Compassion

YOUR STELLAR STYLE
As the twelfth sign of the zodiac, you are the most empathetic and compassionate of all the signs. You're always willing to hear others' troubles and offer your support. But hearing

all sides of a story can leave you feeling as if you're swimming in all directions. And like a fish, you fear confinement and feeling restricted. You are seen as someone who glides about gracefully in social situations. Guided by Neptune, you appear to others as soft-spoken and completely creative.

WHAT YOU NEED TO SUCCEED

You need more solitude than most people do. You're highly sensitive to what others say so it's important for you to hang out with only the most positive people. You have a wide-eyed and optimistic outlook on life and the last thing you need is to be around people who want to reel you into a net of negative energy. When you feel you matter to others as much as they matter to you, you give 110 percent. Approval is important to you and when you feel the support of your family and friends, you often burst through old boundaries and set new goals for yourself.

FAMILY MATTERS

So you feel their pain. That doesn't mean you need to take on others' troubles regardless of whether they affect you or not. Caring about the well-being of others is commendable but taking on their burdens makes no sense. Empathy is an awesome trait but sometimes you feel the pain of others so strongly that you drain all your own energy. Try to maintain a safer distance. Strange as it may seem to someone as sympathetic as you, deciding to dabble in a little bit of emotional detachment may actually lead to a healthier family dynamic.

STUDY STYLES THAT SUIT YOUR SIGN

You love using words and enjoy poetry, plays, and stories. Sign up for an extra English class or consider getting involved in drama. You operate best when you receive lots of encouragement from those around you, so hang with a crowd that's hip to that fact. You're also likely to sink or swim at school depending on how your friends do — if they are high achievers it's likely you'll follow suit, but if they're slackers then you may find it difficult to get motivated yourself. Align yourself with the hard workers for best results.

WHAT MAKES YOU A SOCIAL STAR

You bring a warm and happy vibe to any occasion. You take people at face value and don't try to influence them or change their views.

You tend to drift off into a dreamy world but if someone mentions something remotely nostalgic or sentimental, you check back in and tears well up in your eyes. Your friends mean the world to you and nothing makes you happier than to feel like you are truly one of the gang.

YOUR HEALTHY ASTRO ATTITUDE
Swim, dive, or take long walks. Workouts that engage your mind as well as your body, such as tai chi, Pilates, and yoga, can help to mellow out your workout repertoire. That way, while your mind is meditating, your body is still benefiting from being put through the paces. Since you're a water sign, try rowing or swimming your way to becoming totally toned.

FUTURE THINK
Fresh air and a peaceful, nonaggressive environment are key components to careers that will click with you. You value your autonomy and would excel as a writer, artist, or professional musician. Hands-on experience matters and you shouldn't rule out occupations that put you near the ocean. Jobs in the fields of marine biology or oceanography are natural

picks for a Pisces. Influencing others through work in advertising or public relations or a job as a photographer or physician are other choices that make sense for your sign.

ASTRO ADVICE ALWAYS
Challenge your old way of doing things.
Let your imagination run wild.
Pay attention to what a close friend has to say.
Surround yourself with people who make you feel secure.

WINNING MOVES
FOR THE MONTHS AHEAD
Make your mark on the world by showing off one of your greatest gifts. A performance or sports event will give you the confidence you need to believe in your abilities and push yourself to excel even more. Stay focused and go for the prize!

Elements
of You

Fire, Earth, Air, Water

———————

*E*ach of the twelve signs of the zodiac belongs to a particular group. Basically, there are four teams and your sign is on one of 'em. Think of it as another piece to help you put together your personal astrological puzzle. Hey, this element stuff could provide the crucial clue that'll help you solve the mystery of why your best friend is so much like you even though she doesn't share your sign. Could be she's in your element!

FIRE
(Aries, Leo, Sagittarius)

Fire means fuel. Which means energy. And that adds up to action. Fire sign females are big on getting involved but aren't likely to waste time thinking about the outcome or why things turned out a certain way. Their philosophy? Move on, already. In fact, if you want to get in good with someone born under one of the fire signs, suggest doing something that's active and adventurous.

Buzzwords: energetic and enthusiastic

EARTH
(Taurus, Virgo, Capricorn)

Earth sign individuals are literally down-to-earth — they have their feet firmly planted on the ground. Practical and pragmatic, they're not the people to turn to for advice when you're considering doing something that's risky. You may want to keep those head-in-the-clouds, dreamy ideas from your conventional and conservative earth sign friends.

Buzzwords: practical and secure

AIR

(Gemini, Libra, Aquarius)

Air sign sisters are superethereal. They're way into dreams, imagination, and out-of-this-world thinking. Innovative and original ideas impress them and they're big on people who share their most out-there thoughts. Totally tolerant, they aren't likely to laugh at even the most outrageous ideas. Free spirits of the zodiac, air sign individuals don't like to be tied down and need to have the option to change their minds.

Buzzwords: communicative and open

WATER

(Cancer, Scorpio, Pisces)

Water babies are the mind readers of the zodiac. They are forever examining their feelings and often base their opinions of others on their personal insights. If you're comfortable talking about your feelings and sharing the most creative side of yourself, you can make a cosmic connection with your water sign pals.

Buzzwords: intuitive and empathetic

The Friendship Factor

Friend's sign → / Your sign ↓	Aries	Taurus	Gemini	Cancer	Leo	Virgo
Aries	bag	bag	phone	faces	faces	faces
Taurus	bag	bag	bag	faces	faces	bag
Gemini	phone	bag	bag	bag	faces	bag
Cancer	faces	faces	bag	bag	bag	faces
Leo	faces	faces	faces	bag	bag	bag
Virgo	faces	bag	bag	faces	bag	bag
Libra	phone	faces	faces	faces	phone	bag
Scorpio	faces	phone	bag	faces	bag	phone
Sagittarius	faces	bag	phone	faces	faces	bag
Capricorn	faces	faces	faces	phone	faces	faces
Aquarius	phone	faces	phone	faces	phone	bag
Pisces	bag	phone	faces	phone	faces	faces

Find the intersection of your sign and your friends' signs to discover your kind of cosmic connection.

😊😊 - Best Friends Forever

📱 - Awesome Amigas

👜 - Pal Potential

Libra	Scorpio	Sagittarius	Capricorn	Aquarius	Pisces
♎	🦂	🏹	🐐	♒	🐟
📱	😊😊	😊😊	😊😊	📱	👜
😊😊	📱	👜	😊😊	😊😊	📱
😊😊	👜	📱	😊😊	😊😊	😊😊
😊😊	😊😊	😊😊	📱	😊😊	😊😊
📱	👜	😊😊	😊😊	📱	😊😊
👜	📱	👜	😊😊	👜	😊😊
📱	👜	👜	👜	😊😊	👜
👜	👜	👜	📱	😊😊	😊😊
📱	👜	👜	👜	😊😊	😊😊
👜	📱	👜	👜	👜	📱
😊😊	👜	😊😊	👜	👜	👜
👜	😊😊	😊😊	👜	👜	👜
♎	🦂	🏹	🐐	♒	🐟

If you're friends with an Aries: She can be impulsive and impractical, but she's got an imagination that just won't quit. Wherever you go and whatever you do with your Aries amiga, one thing's for sure: It'll be fun. If you want her to be a friend for life, remember that she's a sucker for compliments. The only problem with having an Aries pal is keeping up with her lickety-split pace!

Gifts that'll be hits: red roses, a cute T-shirt, a favorite book, anything personalized with her name, anything that's wrapped up in a really cool way, a cute baseball cap or hat since Aries rules the head. Keep in mind the color for any true-blue Aries is bright, bright red!

If you're friends with a Taurus: Your Taurus pal can be strong-willed and possessive but she's about as loyal as they come. If you have her understanding and the patience to keep up with her occasional stubborn streaks, you've got yourself a forever friend.

Gifts that'll be hits: If your pal has true Taurean tendencies, she's way tuned into her senses. Any gift that can be smelled, tasted, touched, or heard will have her hooked. Think scented shower gel, yummy chocolates, a supersoft sweater, or the latest CD from her favorite musical group. Since Taurus is the sign associated with the throat, a chenille scarf would also be a great gift. As an earth sign, her colors are earthy tones such as greens, browns, and shades of gold.

If you're friends with a Gemini: This girl can be kind of kooky and confusing. Just roll with it. She thrives on contradiction. Her thoughts are free-flowing and can seem to come from left field. But her wacko ramblings are one of the things that make it so much fun to be around her. No question, time spent with a Gemini friend is undeniably entertaining.

Gifts that'll be hits: Since she's the queen of conversation, going with a cute calling card or a bright and colorful telephone/address book would be a sure way to dial up success if you're giving a gift to a Gemini girl. Also, she's got a real love for gadgets, so a new game for her computer or a handheld puzzle is sure to please.

If you're friends with a Cancer: Don't think she's an open book. There are some chapters she'll probably never reveal. She can have ups and downs that take you on a real rollercoaster ride. But she's also a complete charmer. She needs a lot of attention and absolute loyalty from you, but in return you will receive a friendship that's solid and steadfast.

Gifts that'll be hits: Tap into her sentimental streak by adding to that cool collection she's got going on. Or go with a find from a flea market or a small offering from a local antique shop. You can also score major points by giving her, an animal lover of epic proportions, a gift that's actually a present for her favorite pet.

If you're friends with a Leo: A total extrovert, your Leo pal loves to laugh and is into the best of everything. She'll take risks that can make you nervous, but she's always confident she'll come out a winner. Throw compliments her way and realize you've got a loyal, supertrue friend.

Gifts that'll be hits: As long as your gift is something completely outrageous, your Leo friend will love it. See, the sky's the limit when it comes to getting the right gift for a Leo. But since you can't exactly charter a jet to London so she can play stand-in for one of the Spice Girls, you're better off doing some special investigative work and coming up with a creative alternative. Something on a smaller scale but still totally original that says, "I was totally thinking of you." She's way into her hair, so a cool clip or funky little brush would be a nice offering.

If you're friends with a Virgo: Hanging out with a Virgo pal means you're going to be checking out all kinds of new things. Curious by nature, she'll clue you in to new ideas and events. Not one to hook up with many different people, if she's friends with you, she's gonna be on your social calendar for years to come.

Gifts that'll be hits: If she's true to her type, your Virgo pal loves anything intricate. A beaded bracelet or a small carved box for storing her earrings are good bets. Craft supplies would be a nice gift for a Virgo, too, since she loves to use her hands to create new things. Her colors are blue and green.

If you're friends with a Libra: Born under the sign of the scales, your Libra friend strives for harmony and balance in her life. She's a patient pal and loves to shop. Friendship for her is a serious thing. Don't be surprised if she's always a special someone in your life.

Gifts that'll be hits: That Libra in your life is sure to love anything that makes the most of her wardrobe. She loves clothes and a cute, pastel-colored cardigan will make her happy. A framed photo of the two of you or of your whole pack of pals is also something she'd love to receive 'cause she's big on celebrating friendship.

If you're friends with a Scorpio: Being friends with an emotional and unpredictable Scorpio means there's rarely a dull moment. Remember that while she never forgets a thoughtful gesture on your part, she's also unlikely to forget a social snub. Nothing holds her back, so be prepared for some exciting adventures. **Gifts that'll be hits:** Play into her mysterious personality by giving her something that she needs to solve. A puzzle or a mystery book would make her day. Think magic, intrigue, and suspense.

If you're friends with a Sagittarius: Beyond kind, a Sag friend will make you feel like the center of the universe when you're with her. But don't be deceived — she's actually close to lots of people. Being friends with you doesn't mean she's going to give up being friends with everyone else. Give her lots of space to do her own thing and you'll have a friendship that'll go on for years to come.

Gifts that'll be hits: Supersporty, a Sag would love anything that helps her excel in her game. Her color is purple. A plant or anything to do with gardening are also gifts that are sure to please your Sag pal.

If you're friends with a Capricorn: When she suggests something fun to do, sign on. If you can keep up with a Cap, she'll wanna hang with you all the time. She loves to be with people who are as fast-paced as she is. Beware that if you can't keep up with her pace, she may want to burst free from the constraints of a pairing that seems to be holding her back.

Gifts that'll be hits: A practical present is what makes the most sense for Caps. Forget frivolous! A gift that will help your Capricorn friend get ahead would be appreciated. A planner or datebook are examples. If you decide to go with something for her to wear, remember conservative is the name of the game. She's not about flash.

If you're friends with an Aquarius: Generous and open, an Aquarian friend is always interested in what's going on in your world. Sometimes shy, she may wait for you to make the first moves in setting up stuff to do. She responds to subtle suggestions and is capable of being one of the kindest friends you could hope to have.

Gifts that'll be hits: A computer game or a funky mouse pad will win over your Water Bearer bud. She's always looking to the future, so your best bet is to think ahead — as in the next millennium! Cool colors for her are sky blue or silver.

If you're friends with a Pisces: Since the symbol of Pisces is two fishes swimming in opposite directions, you'll find that your Pisces pal is frequently pulled down different paths. She's impulsive and sometimes can seem unstable. She's very loyal and will even put up with behavior that others might consider unforgivable. But don't expect her to always be around for you. She's easily influenced by changing social conditions and tends to go with the flow, wherever it may take her.

Gifts that'll be hits: Plugged into her emotions, a Pisces pal would appreciate a book of poetry (think Jewel), tickets to a super-sentimental movie, or an elegant blank journal. Pisces is ruled by the feet, so a pair of fuzzy socks or funky slippers are great gift choices.

Your
Moon Sign

Moon Sign Magic:
Clues to the More Mysterious You

———◆·◆———

So, you think you've just about figured yourself out based on your astro sign? Puh-leeze! There's more to solving your astro profile than that! While your astrological, or sun, sign says some things about your public persona, another factor worth focusing on is your moon sign. Your moon sign influences the innermost you, the more private side of your personality. Think of it as the element that influences your secret self, the you only a few of your closest friends know about.

To find out what your moon sign is, check out the charts on pages 96–119. All you have to do is: In the section that covers the year in which you were born (1987, 1988, 1989), find the month in which you were born, then the day. Look down that column until you come to an astro sign — this is your moon sign! Once you've got that vital tidbit of information, here's how to latch on to your lunar lowdown:

If you were born under an Aries moon: You're independent and filled with self-determination. You focus your life around yourself. And while that might sound selfish, it helps you to excel as a driven and dynamic person. You tend to want your own way and you're not big on being babied. Make a point of slowing down long enough to avoid racing off and making sudden decisions that you'll end up regretting.

If you were born under a Taurus moon: A natural nurturer, you're seen as the earth mother of your social circle. You like to provide physical and emotional comfort to those who are troubled. You need stability in your life and always strive to create a harmonious home life. You also scope out any problems that may arise with your friends before things flare up.

If you were born under a Gemini moon:
It can be hard for you to spend tons of time caring for others because it drains you of energy. You like to be free to move along on your merry way. You're a fun-loving person who thrives on being surrounded by lots of friends. Your ideal scene is being able to experience tons of social contact without having to bother with lots of emotional upheavals.

If you were born under a Cancer moon:
You love being with family and friends. Building a foundation of social support matters to you. You're very emotional and sensitive to what others say about you. You strive to make all your relationships work. Emotional connections matter to you more than just about anything.

If you were born under a Leo moon:
You have a need to be recognized and appreciated. You tend to be outgoing and love hanging out with your friends. You like doing nice things for people; in fact, you're into making grand, showy gestures when it comes to those you care about most. You strive to be

the best you can be and you enjoy sharing your finest qualities with others.

If you were born under a Virgo moon:
A bit of a perfectionist, you try to create complete order in your life. Give it up. Instead, try to listen to others and help them out without coming across as too critical. As a rule, people aren't up for being molded into something you want them to be, so put the Play-Doh away and get to know people instead.

If you were born under a Libra moon:
You seek out harmonious social situations. If people are arguing, you steer clear. You're seen as the one who will patch things up between people when tempers flare. Confrontations and hostility cause you to crumble. To you, compromise isn't a cop-out but a means of keeping the peace no matter what the cost.

If you were born under a Scorpio moon:
Your innermost self is fairly intense. You are deeply emotional and though you may hide this side of yourself from even those who know you best, you are passionate about your

connections to others. You're a strong individual who operates with the knowledge that this strength is what fuels your reserve tank and keeps you going.

If you were born under a Sagittarius moon:

You enjoy socializing but your need for connection with others may not be as strong as you let on. You can cope pretty well when you're left on your own. But by and large, being close to female friends is really important.

If you were born under a Capricorn moon:

Your secret self can be your worst critic because it taps into the side of you that really wants more order, discipline, and practical behavior in your life. Let your cuddly, nurturing side come through when you feel you're being influenced too strongly by your moon sign practicality.

If you were born under an Aquarius moon:

With your moon in Aquarius, you can relate to just about everyone on the planet. Your need to heal society's ills and your desire to strive for changes that will benefit society guide the inner you. You want to help the world, but just be sure you don't let your idealistic views get in the way of interacting with others.

If you were born under a Pisces moon: Your inner self causes you to totally empathize with everyone around you and place less emphasis on the issues in your own life. While you're sympathetic and nurturing, you also have the amazing ability to step outside yourself and see things from a different perspective. This makes you a devoted friend.

MOON SIGNS

1987

JANUARY

	1	2	3	4	5	6	7	8	9	10	11	12	13	14
Aries						♈	♈	♈						
Taurus									♉	♉				
Gemini											♊	♊	♊	
Cancer														♋
Leo														
Virgo														
Libra														
Scorpio														
Sagittarius														
Capricorn	♑													
Aquarius		♒	♒											
Pisces				♓	♓									

FEBRUARY

	1	2	3	4	5	6	7	8	9	10	11	12	13	14
Aries			♈	♈										
Taurus					♉	♉								
Gemini							♊	♊	♊					
Cancer										♋	♋			
Leo												♌	♌	♌
Virgo														
Libra														
Scorpio														
Sagittarius														
Capricorn														
Aquarius														
Pisces	♓	♓												

MARCH

	1	2	3	4	5	6	7	8	9	10	11	12	13	14
Aries		♈	♈											
Taurus				♉	♉	♉								
Gemini							♊	♊						
Cancer									♋	♋	♋			
Leo												♌	♌	
Virgo														♍
Libra														
Scorpio														
Sagittarius														
Capricorn														
Aquarius														
Pisces	♓													

To figure out how to use this chart, check out the instructions on pages 90–91.

JANUARY

15	16	17	18	19	20	21	22	23	24	25	26	27	28	29	30	31
♋																
	♌	♌	♌													
				♍	♍											
						♎	♎									
								♏	♏							
										♐	♐					
												♑	♑			
														♒	♒	
																♓

FEBRUARY

15	16	17	18	19	20	21	22	23	24	25	26	27	28
♍	♍												
		♎	♎										
				♏	♏	♏							
							♐	♐					
									♑	♑			
											♒	♒	
													♓

MARCH

15	16	17	18	19	20	21	22	23	24	25	26	27	28	29	30	31
														♈	♈	♈
♍																
	♎	♎	♎													
				♏	♏											
						♐	♐									
								♑	♑							
										♒	♒					
												♓	♓			

1987 APRIL

	1	2	3	4	5	6	7	8	9	10	11	12	13	14
Aries														
Taurus	♉	♉												
Gemini			♊	♊										
Cancer					♋	♋	♋							
Leo								♌	♌					
Virgo										♍	♍	♍		
Libra													♎	♎
Scorpio														
Sagittarius														
Capricorn														
Aquarius														
Pisces														

MAY

	1	2	3	4	5	6	7	8	9	10	11	12	13	14
Aries														
Taurus														
Gemini	♊	♊												
Cancer			♋	♋										
Leo					♌	♌	♌							
Virgo								♍	♍					
Libra										♎	♎			
Scorpio												♏	♏	♏
Sagittarius														
Capricorn														
Aquarius														
Pisces														

JUNE

	1	2	3	4	5	6	7	8	9	10	11	12	13	14
Aries														
Taurus														
Gemini														
Cancer	♋													
Leo		♌	♌											
Virgo				♍	♍	♍								
Libra							♎	♎						
Scorpio									♏	♏				
Sagittarius											♐	♐		
Capricorn													♑	♑
Aquarius														
Pisces														

APRIL

15	16	17	18	19	20	21	22	23	24	25	26	27	28	29	30
											♈	♈			
													♉	♉	
															♊
♏	♏														
		♐	♐												
				♑	♑										
						♒	♒	♒							
									♓	♓					

MAY

15	16	17	18	19	20	21	22	23	24	25	26	27	28	29	30	31
								♈	♈							
										♉	♉	♉				
													♊	♊		
															♋	♋
♐	♐															
		♑	♑													
				♒	♒											
						♓	♓									

JUNE

15	16	17	18	19	20	21	22	23	24	25	26	27	28	29	30
				♈	♈										
						♉	♉	♉							
									♊	♊					
											♋	♋	♋		
														♌	♌
♒	♒														
		♓	♓												

1987

JULY

	1	2	3	4	5	6	7	8	9	10	11	12	13	14
Aries														
Taurus														
Gemini														
Cancer														
Leo														
Virgo	♍	♍	♍											
Libra				♎	♎									
Scorpio						♏	♏							
Sagittarius								♐	♐					
Capricorn										♑	♑			
Aquarius												♒	♒	
Pisces														♓

AUGUST

	1	2	3	4	5	6	7	8	9	10	11	12	13	14
Aries													♈	♈
Taurus														
Gemini														
Cancer														
Leo														
Virgo														
Libra	♎	♎												
Scorpio			♏	♏										
Sagittarius					♐	♐								
Capricorn							♑	♑						
Aquarius									♒	♒				
Pisces											♓	♓		

SEPTEMBER

	1	2	3	4	5	6	7	8	9	10	11	12	13	14
Aries									♈	♈				
Taurus											♉	♉	♉	
Gemini														♊
Cancer														
Leo														
Virgo														
Libra														
Scorpio														
Sagittarius	♐	♐												
Capricorn			♑	♑										
Aquarius					♒	♒								
Pisces							♓	♓						

JULY

15	16	17	18	19	20	21	22	23	24	25	26	27	28	29	30	31
	♈	♈	♈													
				♉	♉											
						♊	♊	♊								
									♋	♋						
											♌	♌	♌			
														♍	♍	
																♎
♓																

AUGUST

15	16	17	18	19	20	21	22	23	24	25	26	27	28	29	30	31
♉	♉															
		♊	♊	♊												
					♋	♋										
							♌	♌	♌							
										♍	♍					
												♎	♎	♎		
															♏	♏

SEPTEMBER

15	16	17	18	19	20	21	22	23	24	25	26	27	28	29	30
♊															
	♋	♋	♋												
				♌	♌										
						♍	♍	♍							
									♎	♎					
											♏	♏			
													♐	♐	
															♑

1987

OCTOBER

	1	2	3	4	5	6	7	8	9	10	11	12	13	14
Aries							♈	♈						
Taurus									♉	♉				
Gemini											♊	♊		
Cancer													♋	♋
Leo														
Virgo														
Libra														
Scorpio														
Sagittarius														
Capricorn	♑	♑												
Aquarius			♒	♒										
Pisces					♓	♓								

NOVEMBER

	1	2	3	4	5	6	7	8	9	10	11	12	13	14
Aries			♈	♈										
Taurus					♉	♉								
Gemini							♊	♊	♊					
Cancer										♋	♋			
Leo												♌	♌	♌
Virgo														
Libra														
Scorpio														
Sagittarius														
Capricorn														
Aquarius														
Pisces	♓	♓												

DECEMBER

	1	2	3	4	5	6	7	8	9	10	11	12	13	14
Aries	♈	♈												
Taurus			♉	♉										
Gemini					♊	♊								
Cancer							♋	♋	♋					
Leo										♌	♌			
Virgo												♍	♍	♍
Libra														
Scorpio														
Sagittarius														
Capricorn														
Aquarius														
Pisces														

OCTOBER

15	16	17	18	19	20	21	22	23	24	25	26	27	28	29	30	31
♋																
	♌	♌	♌													
				♍	♍											
						♎	♎									
								♏	♏	♏						
											♐	♐				
													♑	♑		
															♒	♒

NOVEMBER

15	16	17	18	19	20	21	22	23	24	25	26	27	28	29	30
															♈
♍	♍														
		♎	♎	♎											
					♏	♏									
							♐	♐							
									♑	♑					
											♒	♒			
													♓	♓	

DECEMBER

15	16	17	18	19	20	21	22	23	24	25	26	27	28	29	30	31
													♈	♈		
															♉	♉
♎	♎															
		♏	♏													
				♐	♐											
						♑	♑									
								♒	♒							
										♓	♓	♓				

1988

JANUARY

	1	2	3	4	5	6	7	8	9	10	11	12	13	14
Aries														
Taurus														
Gemini	♊	♊												
Cancer			♋	♋	♋									
Leo						♌	♌							
Virgo								♍	♍	♍				
Libra											♎	♎		
Scorpio													♏	♏
Sagittarius														
Capricorn														
Aquarius														
Pisces														

FEBRUARY

	1	2	3	4	5	6	7	8	9	10	11	12	13	14
Aries														
Taurus														
Gemini														
Cancer	♋													
Leo		♌	♌	♌										
Virgo						♍	♍							
Libra								♎	♎	♎				
Scorpio										♏	♏			
Sagittarius												♐	♐	
Capricorn														♑
Aquarius														
Pisces														

MARCH

	1	2	3	4	5	6	7	8	9	10	11	12	13	14
Aries														
Taurus														
Gemini														
Cancer														
Leo	♌	♌												
Virgo			♍	♍	♍									
Libra						♎	♎							
Scorpio								♏	♏					
Sagittarius										♐	♐	♐		
Capricorn													♑	♑
Aquarius														
Pisces														

JANUARY

15	16	17	18	19	20	21	22	23	24	25	26	27	28	29	30	31
									♈	♈						
											♉	♉				
													♊	♊	♊	
																♋
♏																
	♐	♐														
			♑	♑												
					♒	♒										
							♓	♓								

FEBRUARY

15	16	17	18	19	20	21	22	23	24	25	26	27	28	29
					♈	♈								
							♉	♉	♉					
										♊	♊			
												♋	♋	
														♌
♑														
	♒	♒												
			♓	♓										

MARCH

15	16	17	18	19	20	21	22	23	24	25	26	27	28	29	30	31
				♈	♈											
						♉	♉									
								♊	♊							
										♋	♋	♋				
													♌	♌		
															♍	♍
♒	♒															
		♓	♓													

1988

APRIL

	1	2	3	4	5	6	7	8	9	10	11	12	13	14
Aries														
Taurus														
Gemini														
Cancer														
Leo														
Virgo	♍													
Libra		♎	♎											
Scorpio				♏	♏	♏								
Sagittarius							♐	♐						
Capricorn									♑	♑				
Aquarius											♒	♒		
Pisces													♓	♓

MAY

	1	2	3	4	5	6	7	8	9	10	11	12	13	14
Aries												♈	♈	♈
Taurus														
Gemini														
Cancer														
Leo														
Virgo														
Libra	♎													
Scorpio		♏	♏											
Sagittarius				♐	♐									
Capricorn						♑	♑							
Aquarius								♒	♒					
Pisces										♓	♓			

JUNE

	1	2	3	4	5	6	7	8	9	10	11	12	13	14
Aries									♈	♈				
Taurus											♉	♉		
Gemini													♊	♊
Cancer														
Leo														
Virgo														
Libra														
Scorpio														
Sagittarius	♐													
Capricorn		♑	♑											
Aquarius				♒	♒	♒								
Pisces							♓	♓						

APRIL

15	16	17	18	19	20	21	22	23	24	25	26	27	28	29	30
♈	♈														
		♉	♉												
				♊	♊	♊									
							♋	♋							
									♌	♌	♌				
												♍	♍		
														♎	♎

MAY

15	16	17	18	19	20	21	22	23	24	25	26	27	28	29	30	31
♉	♉															
		♊	♊													
				♋	♋											
						♌	♌	♌								
									♍	♍						
											♎	♎	♎			
														♏	♏	
																♐

JUNE

15	16	17	18	19	20	21	22	23	24	25	26	27	28	29	30
♋	♋	♋													
			♌	♌											
					♍	♍	♍								
								♎	♎						
										♏	♏	♏			
													♐	♐	
															♑

1988   JULY

	1	2	3	4	5	6	7	8	9	10	11	12	13	14
Aries						♈	♈							
Taurus								♉	♉					
Gemini										♊	♊	♊		
Cancer													♋	♋
Leo														
Virgo														
Libra														
Scorpio														
Sagittarius														
Capricorn	♑													
Aquarius		♒	♒											
Pisces				♓	♓									

AUGUST

	1	2	3	4	5	6	7	8	9	10	11	12	13	14
Aries		♈	♈											
Taurus				♉	♉	♉								
Gemini							♊	♊						
Cancer									♋	♋				
Leo											♌	♌	♌	
Virgo														♍
Libra														
Scorpio														
Sagittarius														
Capricorn														
Aquarius														
Pisces	♓													

SEPTEMBER

	1	2	3	4	5	6	7	8	9	10	11	12	13	14
Aries														
Taurus	♉	♉												
Gemini			♊	♊										
Cancer					♋	♋	♋							
Leo								♌	♌					
Virgo										♍	♍	♍		
Libra													♎	♎
Scorpio														
Sagittarius														
Capricorn														
Aquarius														
Pisces														

JULY

15	16	17	18	19	20	21	22	23	24	25	26	27	28	29	30	31
♌	♌	♌														
			♍	♍												
					♎	♎	♎									
								♏	♏							
										♐	♐					
												♑	♑			
														♒	♒	
																♓

AUGUST

15	16	17	18	19	20	21	22	23	24	25	26	27	28	29	30	31
															♈	♈
♍																
	♎	♎	♎													
				♏	♏											
						♐	♐	♐								
									♑	♑						
											♒	♒				
													♓	♓		

SEPTEMBER

15	16	17	18	19	20	21	22	23	24	25	26	27	28	29	30
									♈	♈					
											♉	♉			
													♊		
♏	♏	♏													
			♐	♐											
					♑	♑									
							♒	♒							
									♓	♓					

1988

OCTOBER

	1	2	3	4	5	6	7	8	9	10	11	12	13	14
Aries														
Taurus														
Gemini	♊													
Cancer		♋	♋	♋										
Leo					♌	♌								
Virgo							♍	♍	♍					
Libra										♎	♎			
Scorpio												♏	♏	♏
Sagittarius														
Capricorn														
Aquarius														
Pisces														

NOVEMBER

	1	2	3	4	5	6	7	8	9	10	11	12	13	14
Aries														
Taurus														
Gemini														
Cancer														
Leo	♌	♌	♌											
Virgo				♍	♍									
Libra						♎	♎	♎						
Scorpio									♏	♏				
Sagittarius											♐	♐		
Capricorn													♑	♑
Aquarius														
Pisces														

DECEMBER

	1	2	3	4	5	6	7	8	9	10	11	12	13	14
Aries														
Taurus														
Gemini														
Cancer														
Leo														
Virgo	♍	♍												
Libra			♎	♎	♎									
Scorpio						♏	♏							
Sagittarius								♐	♐	♐				
Capricorn											♑	♑		
Aquarius													♒	♒
Pisces														

OCTOBER

15	16	17	18	19	20	21	22	23	24	25	26	27	28	29	30	31
									♈	♈						
											♉	♉				
													♊	♊		
															♋	♋
♐	♐															
		♑	♑													
				♒	♒											
						♓	♓	♓								

NOVEMBER

15	16	17	18	19	20	21	22	23	24	25	26	27	28	29	30
					♈	♈									
							♉	♉							
									♊	♊					
											♋	♋			
													♌	♌	
															♍
♑															
	♒	♒													
			♓	♓											

DECEMBER

15	16	17	18	19	20	21	22	23	24	25	26	27	28	29	30	31
	♈	♈														
			♉	♉												
					♊	♊	♊									
									♋	♋						
											♌	♌				
													♍	♍	♍	
																♎
♓	♓															

JANUARY

	1	2	3	4	5	6	7	8	9	10	11	12	13	14
Aries													♈	♈
Taurus														
Gemini														
Cancer														
Leo														
Virgo														
Libra	♎													
Scorpio		♏	♏	♏										
Sagittarius					♐	♐								
Capricorn							♑	♑						
Aquarius									♒	♒				
Pisces											♓	♓		

FEBRUARY

	1	2	3	4	5	6	7	8	9	10	11	12	13	14
Aries										♈	♈			
Taurus												♉	♉	
Gemini														♊
Cancer														
Leo														
Virgo														
Libra														
Scorpio														
Sagittarius	♐	♐												
Capricorn			♑	♑	♑									
Aquarius						♒	♒							
Pisces								♓	♓					

MARCH

	1	2	3	4	5	6	7	8	9	10	11	12	13	14
Aries									♈	♈				
Taurus											♉	♉		
Gemini													♊	♊
Cancer														
Leo														
Virgo														
Libra														
Scorpio														
Sagittarius	♐	♐												
Capricorn			♑	♑										
Aquarius					♒	♒								
Pisces							♓	♓						

JANUARY

15	16	17	18	19	20	21	22	23	24	25	26	27	28	29	30	31
♉	♉	♉														
			♊	♊												
					♋	♋										
							♌	♌	♌							
										♍	♍					
												♎	♎	♎		
															♏	♏

FEBRUARY

15	16	17	18	19	20	21	22	23	24	25	26	27	28
♊													
	♋	♋											
			♌	♌	♌								
						♍	♍						
								♎	♎	♎			
											♏	♏	
													♐

MARCH

15	16	17	18	19	20	21	22	23	24	25	26	27	28	29	30	31
♋	♋	♋														
			♌	♌												
					♍	♍	♍									
								♎	♎							
										♏	♏	♏				
													♐	♐		
															♑	♑

1989

APRIL

	1	2	3	4	5	6	7	8	9	10	11	12	13	14
Aries						♈	♈							
Taurus								♉	♉					
Gemini										♊	♊			
Cancer												♋	♋	
Leo														♌
Virgo														
Libra														
Scorpio														
Sagittarius														
Capricorn														
Aquarius	♒	♒	♒											
Pisces				♓	♓									

MAY

	1	2	3	4	5	6	7	8	9	10	11	12	13	14
Aries			♈	♈										
Taurus					♉	♉								
Gemini							♊	♊						
Cancer									♋	♋				
Leo											♌	♌	♌	
Virgo														♍
Libra														
Scorpio														
Sagittarius														
Capricorn														
Aquarius														
Pisces	♓	♓												

JUNE

	1	2	3	4	5	6	7	8	9	10	11	12	13	14
Aries														
Taurus	♉	♉												
Gemini			♊	♊										
Cancer					♋	♋	♋							
Leo								♌	♌					
Virgo										♍	♍	♍		
Libra													♎	♎
Scorpio														
Sagittarius														
Capricorn														
Aquarius														
Pisces														

APRIL

15	16	17	18	19	20	21	22	23	24	25	26	27	28	29	30
♌															
	♍	♍	♍												
				♎	♎	♎									
							♏	♏							
									♐	♐					
											♑	♑	♑		
														♒	♒

MAY

15	16	17	18	19	20	21	22	23	24	25	26	27	28	29	30	31
															♈	♈
♍																
	♎	♎	♎													
				♏	♏											
						♐	♐	♐								
									♑	♑						
											♒	♒				
													♓	♓		

JUNE

15	16	17	18	19	20	21	22	23	24	25	26	27	28	29	30
												♈	♈		
														♉	♉
♏	♏	♏													
			♐	♐											
					♑	♑									
							♒	♒							
									♓	♓	♓				

1989

JULY

	1	2	3	4	5	6	7	8	9	10	11	12	13	14
Aries														
Taurus														
Gemini	♊	♊												
Cancer			♋	♋										
Leo					♌	♌								
Virgo							♍	♍	♍					
Libra										♎	♎			
Scorpio												♏	♏	♏
Sagittarius														
Capricorn														
Aquarius														
Pisces														

AUGUST

	1	2	3	4	5	6	7	8	9	10	11	12	13	14
Aries														
Taurus														
Gemini														
Cancer														
Leo	♌	♌	♌											
Virgo				♍	♍									
Libra						♎	♎	♎						
Scorpio									♏	♏				
Sagittarius											♐	♐	♐	
Capricorn														♑
Aquarius														
Pisces														

SEPTEMBER

	1	2	3	4	5	6	7	8	9	10	11	12	13	14
Aries														
Taurus														
Gemini														
Cancer														
Leo														
Virgo	♍	♍												
Libra			♎	♎										
Scorpio					♏	♏	♏							
Sagittarius								♐	♐					
Capricorn										♑	♑			
Aquarius												♒	♒	
Pisces														♓

116

JULY

15	16	17	18	19	20	21	22	23	24	25	26	27	28	29	30	31
									♈	♈						
											♉	♉				
													♊	♊		
															♋	♋
♐	♐															
		♑	♑													
				♒	♒	♒										
							♓	♓								

AUGUST

15	16	17	18	19	20	21	22	23	24	25	26	27	28	29	30	31
					♈	♈										
							♉	♉								
									♊	♊						
											♋	♋	♋			
														♌	♌	
																♍
♑																
	♒	♒														
			♓	♓												

SEPTEMBER

15	16	17	18	19	20	21	22	23	24	25	26	27	28	29	30
	♈	♈													
			♉	♉											
					♊	♊	♊								
								♋	♋						
										♌	♌				
												♍	♍	♍	
															♎
♓															

1989

OCTOBER

	1	2	3	4	5	6	7	8	9	10	11	12	13	14
Aries														♈
Taurus														
Gemini														
Cancer														
Leo														
Virgo														
Libra	♎													
Scorpio		♏	♏	♏										
Sagittarius					♐	♐								
Capricorn							♑	♑	♑					
Aquarius										♒	♒			
Pisces												♓	♓	

NOVEMBER

	1	2	3	4	5	6	7	8	9	10	11	12	13	14
Aries										♈	♈			
Taurus												♉	♉	
Gemini														♊
Cancer														
Leo														
Virgo														
Libra														
Scorpio														
Sagittarius	♐	♐	♐											
Capricorn				♑	♑									
Aquarius						♒	♒							
Pisces								♓	♓					

DECEMBER

	1	2	3	4	5	6	7	8	9	10	11	12	13	14
Aries								♈	♈					
Taurus										♉	♉			
Gemini												♊	♊	
Cancer														♋
Leo														
Virgo														
Libra														
Scorpio														
Sagittarius														
Capricorn	♑	♑												
Aquarius			♒	♒										
Pisces					♓	♓	♓							

OCTOBER

15	16	17	18	19	20	21	22	23	24	25	26	27	28	29	30	31
♈																
	♉	♉														
			♊	♊												
					♋	♋										
							♌	♌	♌							
										♍	♍					
												♎	♎	♎		
															♏	♏

NOVEMBER

15	16	17	18	19	20	21	22	23	24	25	26	27	28	29	30
♊															
	♋	♋													
			♌	♌	♌										
						♍	♍								
								♎	♎	♎					
											♏	♏			
													♐	♐	♐

DECEMBER

15	16	17	18	19	20	21	22	23	24	25	26	27	28	29	30	31
♋																
	♌	♌														
			♍	♍	♍											
						♎	♎									
								♏	♏	♏						
											♐	♐				
													♑	♑		
															♒	♒

CELEBRITY SIGNS
Which Stars Share Your Sign?

Aries
Mariah Carey
Claire Danes
Jennie Garth
Sarah Michelle Gellar
Melissa Joan Hart

Taurus
David Boreanaz
George Clooney
Janet Jackson
Tori Spelling
Uma Thurman

Gemini
Joshua Jackson
Jewel
Nicole Kidman
Alanis Morissette
Prince William
Scott Wolf

Cancer
Tom Cruise
Matthew Fox
Courtney Love
Liv Tyler

Leo
Ben Affleck
Halle Berry
Sandra Bullock
David Duchovny
Matt LeBlanc
Madonna

Virgo
Fiona Apple
Cameron Diaz
James Marsden
Jason Priestley
Adam Sandler
Jonathan Taylor Thomas
Michelle Williams

Check out these fab (and way famous) folks
who share your sign.

Libra
Neve Campbell
Lacey Chabert
Matt Damon
Martina Hingis
Alicia Silverstone
Will Smith
Gwen Stefani
Kate Winslet

Scorpio
Leonardo DiCaprio
Calista Flockhart
Ethan Hawke
Monica
Julia Roberts
Winona Ryder

Sagittarius
Tyra Banks
Brendan Fraser
Katie Holmes
Alyssa Milano
Brad Pitt

Capricorn
Nicolas Cage
Jared Leto
Kate Moss
Tiger Woods

Aquarius
Jennifer Aniston
Brandy
Nick Carter
Matt Dillon
Minnie Driver
Christina Ricci
Tiffani-Amber Thiessen

Pisces
Drew Barrymore
Chelsea Clinton
Cindy Crawford
Jennifer Love Hewitt
Andrew Shue
James Van Der Beek

CELEB MOON SIGNS

Aries moon
Minnie Driver

Libra moon
Kate Winslet

Taurus moon
Monica

Scorpio moon
Kate Moss

Gemini moon
Martina Hingis

Sagittarius moon
Jennifer Love Hewitt

Cancer moon
Gwen Stefani

Capricorn moon
Liv Tyler

Leo moon
Katie Holmes

Aquarius moon
Calista Flockhart

Virgo moon
Fiona Apple

Pisces moon
Sarah Michelle Gellar

Chinese Astrology

Do your friends think you're a real rat? Ever been told you're a snake? Hey, don't get upset. It could be that someone's clued in to your Chinese astrological sign. Here's the deal. In addition to your zodiac sign, you also have a Chinese astro sign that's based on the year you were born.

The origin of the Chinese zodiac is believed to trace back to a legend about Buddha. Seems the Enlightened One asked all the animals to come hang out with him, but a bunch of them were no-shows. To thank the twelve animals that decided to stop by, he named a year after each of them. To find out which animal sign you were born under, check out the chart below. Then see how your animal magnetism influences what you love and what you loathe.

There are twelve animals (rat, ox, tiger, rabbit, dragon, snake, horse, goat, monkey, rooster, dog, and pig) and they always appear in the same order. The same animal cycle repeats itself every dozen years. To find your sign, look up the year of your birth in the first column. Or you can also find out what animal sign rules your friends and family members. If you were born in January or February, be sure to carefully check out the date the Chinese lunar year actually began to find your correct animal sign.

1982	Jan. 25, 1982–Feb. 12, 1983	**Dog**
1983	Feb. 13, 1983–Feb. 1, 1984	**Pig**
1984	Feb. 2, 1984–Feb. 19, 1985	**Rat**
1985	Feb. 20, 1985–Feb. 8, 1986	**Ox**
1986	Feb. 9, 1986–Jan. 28, 1987	**Tiger**
1987	Jan. 29, 1987–Feb. 16, 1988	**Rabbit**
1988	Feb. 17, 1988–Feb. 5, 1989	**Dragon**
1989	Feb. 6, 1989–Jan. 26, 1990	**Snake**
1990	Jan. 27, 1990–Feb. 14, 1991	**Horse**
1991	Feb. 15, 1991–Feb. 3, 1992	**Goat**
1992	Feb. 4, 1992–Jan. 22, 1993	**Monkey**
1993	Jan. 23, 1993–Feb. 9, 1994	**Rooster**

IF YOU'RE A DOG:

In a word: loyal

Animal attraction: Devoted to your friends, you provide a sense of constancy and loyalty in your friendships that your pals find really reassuring.

You love: learning about other cultures, communicating with others, reunions

You loathe: deceit, selfishness, and hypocritical behavior

Famous dogs: stellar leaders of state Winston Churchill and Golda Meir

IF YOU'RE A PIG:

In a word: kind

Animal attraction: You love to indulge and treat yourself to fun things. Your friends love to hang around 'cause you're usually up for anything.

You love: to work as part of a team, the sound of applause, glamorous surroundings

You loathe: confusion, a lack of privacy, possessiveness

Famous pigs from the past: dynamo dancers Fred Astaire and Ginger Rogers

IF YOU'RE A RAT:

In a word: charming

Animal attraction: You come across to others as someone who's very cool. Deep down, you've got lots of feelings floating around that people might not be aware of. Seemingly in complete control, you have a tendency to overanalyze.

You love: being the first to discover something, mysteries, taking risks

You loathe: feeling isolated, having nothing to do, and getting stuck in dull day-in, day-out routines

Famous rats from the past: men of note William Shakespeare and Wolfgang Amadeus Mozart

IF YOU'RE AN OX:

In a word: dependable

Animal attraction: A steadfast friend, you're very loyal and determined to make things right in all of your relationships with others. You're more than willing to put in the hard work that's sometimes necessary to make your friendships first-rate.

You love: to plan ahead, things that are familiar, honoring traditions

You loathe: stressful situations, sudden change, and way-out-of-line behavior
Famous oxen of old: master musicians Handel and Bach

IF YOU'RE A TIGER:

In a word: charismatic
Animal attraction: All about beating boredom, you are the one your friends turn to when life needs a blast of excitement. You're willing to take risks that many others would never consider.
You love: a challenge, big parties and social situations, being in charge
You loathe: being ignored, feeling restrained, taking orders from others
Famous back-in-time tigers: writers Emily Brontë and John Steinbeck

IF YOU'RE A RABBIT:

In a word: peaceful
Animal attraction: Into emotions and providing friends with lots of reassurance and support, you are someone who's seen as sentimental and sensitive.
You love: privacy, solving mysteries, paying attention to details

You loathe: arguments, surprises, and indecisiveness

Famous retro rabbits: brainiacs Marie Curie and Albert Einstein

IF YOU'RE A DRAGON:

In a word: energetic

Animal attraction: Blazing onto the scene with bizarre ideas may strike some people as strange, but you thrive on excitement and making fiery decisions.

You love: giving advice, being in charge, being a champion for change

You loathe: an unwillingness to change, being manipulated, having nothing to do

Famous dragons from decades ago: compassionate crusaders Florence Nightingale and Martin Luther King, Jr.

IF YOU'RE A SNAKE:

In a word: clever

Animal attraction: Supersmart, you're a supportive friend. But you can be seen as someone who is a little too clingy toward her pals. Loosen up that viselike grip!

You love: beautiful landscapes, harmony, seeing things from many perspectives

You loathe: things that seem artificial, superficial behavior, prejudice
Famous snakes: awe-inspiring artists Henri Matisse and Pablo Picasso

IF YOU'RE A HORSE:

In a word: strong
Animal attraction: Charging onto the scene may startle some, but you love to make a bold entrance and gallop into a group conversation. Your strong style is admired by many.
You love: undertaking new projects, feeling like a pioneer, and expressing your emotions
You loathe: silence, criticism, and solitude
Famous historical horses: master musicians Antonio Vivaldi and Ella Fitzgerald

IF YOU'RE A GOAT:

In a word: artistic
Animal attraction: Down-to-earth and grounded, you are the one people often turn to for advice and solid guidance. You provide friends with a security that they are hard-pressed to find elsewhere.
You love: beauty, tranquility, elaborate costumes and fashions
You loathe: being made to choose, routine tasks, critical comments

Famous goats that go way back: women-of-note author Jane Austen and fashion designer Coco Chanel

IF YOU'RE A MONKEY:

In a word: imaginative

Animal attraction: Playful and funny, you love to make people laugh. Forget routine; you've got to stay entertained.

You love: a challenge, dramatic entrances, seeing something in a new way

You loathe: compromising, depending on others, and doing without

Famous monkeys: Hollywood divas Bette Davis and Joan Crawford

IF YOU'RE A ROOSTER:

In a word: honest

Animal attraction: Stylish and dramatic in the way you dress, you are seen as a bit of a scene-stealer.

You love: being the center of attention, making an entrance, receiving praise

You loathe: being the subject of a practical joke, confiding in others, being asked personal questions

Famous roosters: film legends Errol Flynn and Katharine Hepburn

1 2 3

Numerology

**Numerology:
How Does Your
Birth Date Add Up?**

——————◆•◆——————

Not to worry. This isn't math class. But you will need to add up a string of numbers if you want to find your personal number. You figure out your personal number by adding up your birth date. The cool thing about your number is it never changes. To calculate which number counts most for you, you're gonna want to convert all the information about your birth date into a single number. (If you add things up and you've got a double-digit deal, you're not done yet!)

Here's an example:

If you were born on October 21, 1989, first you'd figure out the number for your birth month (October is month 10).

Then you'd add that to your birthday (21).

Then you'd add that to your birth year (1989).

Your equation would look like this:

$1+0+2+1+1+9+8+9=31$

$3+1=4$

Your personal number would be 4.

Got it? Here goes:

IF YOUR PERSONAL NUMBER IS 1:

The number one is considered to be very powerful. Because one represents the beginning, those with a personal number of one maintain kind of a "me first" attitude. You also like to be the center of attention, as in, "I'm number one." On the plus side, you're seen as someone who's happy most of the time, energetic, and romantic. On the negative side, people may sometimes see you as kind of selfish and egotistical. You're the kind of girl who will take charge of the situation. Independent and original, you're seen as a trendsetter, but at your worst, you can be kind of self-centered. And you really hate being told what to do.

132

IF YOUR PERSONAL NUMBER IS 2:

The number two is associated with partnerships and relationships with others. If you are interested in achieving something on your own, keep in mind that you may get the best results from cooperation and teamwork. But beware! On the negative side, two can cause you to be overprotective and irritable! You can't stand chaos and confusion. A natural peacemaker, you're superloyal to your friends. Just be aware that you can come across as kind of moody.

IF YOUR PERSONAL NUMBER IS 3:

The number three is linked to money and good luck! It often focuses on people joining forces to reach a common goal. Just be aware that three can bring with it pessimism and risk taking. The life of the party, you're the kind of girl who introduces herself to just about everybody. You tend to win over everyone with your social style. You're a creative soul but you can be seen as bossy at times.

IF YOUR PERSONAL NUMBER IS 4:

Like the solidness of the four-sided square, the number four represents stability and a solid foundation. Its focus is on accomplishing goals. Seen as a number of advancement and progress, it can also be seen as steadfast and boring. Hardworking and practical, you're so detail-oriented you can drive your friends nuts. Friends trust you in a big way and often turn to you to help them solve their troubles. But don't let your set-in-your-ways style cause you to avoid trying new things.

IF YOUR PERSONAL NUMBER IS 5:

Five focuses on helping others. You are rarely spotted standing still. Always on the go, you're the one who's trying to talk others into trying something superdaring. Just watch out. Some of your friends may think you're superficial at times.

IF YOUR PERSONAL NUMBER IS 6:

Six relates to harmony and tact. If a friend is bumming in a big way, you're the one she's likely to turn to. You're caring and honest and seen as someone with a heart of gold. Just don't hold your friends to superhigh standards. The expectations you set for yourself may not be a fair way of judging your friends.

IF YOUR PERSONAL NUMBER IS 7:

Seven is the number of spirituality and inspiration. You may be seen as a bit of a dreamer.

But it doesn't faze you in the slightest. Always willing to march to the beat of a different drummer, you're open to original and creative ideas. Sensitive and artistic, you sometimes like to spend time on your own. Just be sure those mood swings don't send people running for cover!

IF YOUR PERSONAL NUMBER IS 8:
Eight represents hard work and learning through experience. Organized and way responsible, you like to stand out in a crowd and you usually do. Nothing but the best is the motto you tend to go by. And that's cool, but don't let your concerns about quality mean that you come across as being supercritical. Your strong personality can sometimes strike people as a bit bossy.

IF YOUR PERSONAL NUMBER IS 9:
Nine represents change and growth. It's probably been said a time or two that you come across as wise beyond your years. A really cool characteristic but it can be intimidating. You're passionate about creativity and learning new things, but don't get so wrapped up in your own world and way of doing things that you end up blowing off your buds in the process.

GOOD VIBRATIONS:
The Vitals on Your Vibration Number

Another number of note is your vibration number. It's based on the date you were born. Those born on the:

1st, 10th, 19th, or **28th** of any month have a vibration number of **1.**

2nd, 11th, 20th, or **29th** of any month have a vibration number of **2.**

3rd, 12th, 21st, or **30th** of any month have a vibration number of **3.**

4th, 13th, 22nd, or **31st** of any month have a vibration number of **4.**

5th, 14th, or **23rd,** of any month have a vibration number of **5.**

6th, 15th, or **24th** of any month have a vibration number of **6.**

7th, 16th, or **25th** of any month have a vibration number of **7.**

8th, 17th, or **26th** of any month have a vibration number of **8.**

9th, 18th, or **27th** of any month have a vibration number of **9.**

Check out the following details on jewels, colors, and compatible pals as they relate to your very own vibration number:

IF YOUR VIBRATION NUMBER IS 1:

Your jewels: topaz and emerald
Your colors: purple, golden brown, yellow, and blue
Your most compatible pals have: vibration numbers of 1, 2, 4, 7, or 9.

IF YOUR VIBRATION NUMBER IS 2:

Your jewels: pearls and jade
Your colors: green and ivory
Your most compatible pals have: vibration numbers of 1, 4, or 7.

IF YOUR VIBRATION NUMBER IS 3:

Your jewel: amethyst
Your color: purple
Your most compatible pals have: vibration numbers of 6, 5, 8, or 9.

IF YOUR VIBRATION NUMBER IS 4:

Your jewel: sapphire
Your colors: blues and grays
Your most compatible pals have: vibration numbers of 1, 2, 3, or 7.

IF YOUR VIBRATION NUMBER IS 5:

Your jewel: diamond
Your colors: gray, red, and white
Your most compatible pals have: vibration numbers of 3, 4, 5, or 7.

IF YOUR VIBRATION NUMBER IS 6:

Your jewel: emerald
Your colors: deep green, white, and pink
Your most compatible pals have: vibration numbers of 3, 8, or 9.

IF YOUR VIBRATION NUMBER IS 7:

Your jewels: moonstones and agates
Your colors: yellow, white, and green
Your most compatible pals have: vibration numbers of 1, 2, 4, or 5.

IF YOUR VIBRATION NUMBER IS 8:

Your jewels: sapphires and diamonds
Your colors: blues and purples
Your most compatible pals have: vibration numbers of 1, 3, or 5.

IF YOUR VIBRATION NUMBER IS 9:

Your jewels: rubies and garnets
Your colors: reds and burgundies
Your most compatible pals have: vibration numbers of 1, 3, 5, or 6.

Scope Out More Info

*I*f you were way into the aspects of astrology and numerology presented in this book, then keep on going! You're already on your way to becoming an expert on this totally entertaining and info-packed subject and reading more will help. Another way to keep going is to check out these great Web sites:

http://teen-net.com/horoscopes
Designed especially for teens, this Web site will tell you more about your sign and show you how to get a complete astrological reading.

http://www.chineseastrology.com/wu/index1.html
This site, which has great graphics, shows how the ancient art of Chinese astrology can apply to your life today.

http://www.astrology-numerology.com
What does your name add up to? Find out at this neat numerology site, which will show you how your numbers can add up to success.

By zeroing in on all there is to know about the zodiac, you'll really get to know yourself, your friends, and your family better!